In the fall of 1980, Charles Habib Malek, a distinguished academic, philosopher, and statesman, rose to give the inaugural address at Wheaton College near Chicago for the dedication of the new Billy Graham Center. In his address, he said that the two main tasks of the church were evangelizing or "saving the soul, and saving the mind"—that is, converting people not only spiritually, but also intellectually. He warned that the church was lagging dangerously behind in this second task.

If philosophy and theology raise questions of ultimate reality (metaphysics), knowledge (epistemology), and morals and values (axiology), a basic questions about the subject matter are what is moral knowledge, what is it about, and how is it achieved? The Post-Enlightenment Modern Consciousness Challenge is to provide for debate in the public realm, standards and methods of rational justification by which alternative courses of action can be judged as true or false, just or unjust, rational or irrational, or enlightened or unenlightened. This challenge obligates us to connect rationality and responsibility. But exactly what conditions of rationality apply?

Here is where Stephen Hiemstra's book, Simple Faith, becomes important.

Stephen walks us carefully through this mine-field of thought in a Biblically centered method with clarifying illustrations to address the problem. Simple Faith is not simplistic—simple means stripped to basic elements or foundations. Yet, meditating on its contexts yields rich fruit.

Honorable Rollin A. Van Broekhoven
JD, LLM, DPhil, DLitt, DPS, LLD
Visiting Scholar, University of Oxford Centre for Socio-Legal Studies. Fellow, American Friends of Oxford House (Oxford, UK and Alexandria, VA). Legal & Cultural Consultant, Asian Center for Law and Culture (Beijing, China)

I'm grateful for Stephen's willingness to tackle these important questions. He's written a practical book that will be useful for those who long to deepen their faith.

Rev. Dr. Stephen A. Macchia

Founder & President of Leadership Transformations, Inc. (www. LeadershipTransformations.org). Author of numerous books, including Broken and Whole (InterVarsity Press), Rule of Life (InterVarsity Press), and Becoming A Healthy Disciple (Baker Books).

Stephen is a deeply thoughtful and introspective person, and He loves the Lord beyond measure. I have read all his books, and this one is also exceptional. Rarely, do I find a modern writer that communicates such depth of knowledge, and yet, practical understanding of the Bible. As a pastor, I have personally used his books in discipleship groups. This one is now added. Jesus said, "I will give you the keys of the kingdom of heaven" Matthew 16:19. In the Hebrew vernacular, keys represent knowledge, knowledge brings understanding, understanding brings awareness, awareness brings assurance, assurance strengthens our faith to believe in things that are unseen, and strong faith is required for us to stand in the place of trial and adversity. When the Lord carries us through difficulty, we grow closer to Him, and when we draw close to Him, we are made into His perfect image. Read this book slowly, meditating on each chapter. You will not only be enriched, but you will be transformed and renewed in your journey with the Lord.

Eric Teitelman

Author and Pastor, House of David Ministries (www.TheHouseOfDavid.org)

Also by Stephen W. Hiemstra:

A Christian Guide to Spirituality

Called Along the Way

Everyday Prayers for Everyday People

Life in Tension

Oraciones

Prayers

Prayers of a Life in Tension

Spiritual Trilogy

Una Guía Cristiana a la Espiritualidad

SIMPLE FAITH

Almost Forgotten Winter Path

SIMPLE FAITH

Something Worth Living For

Stephen W. Hiemstra

T2Pneuma Publishers LLC
Centreville, Virginia

SIMPLE FAITH
Something Worth Living For

Names: Hiemstra, Stephen W., author.
Title: Simple faith : something worth living for / Stephen W. Hiemstra.
Description: Centreville, VA: T2Pneuma Publishers LLC, 2019.
Identifiers: LCCN 2019900447 | ISBN 978-1-942199-23-6 (pbk.) | 978-1-942199-35-9 (Kindle) | 978-1-942199-50-2 (epub)
Subjects: LCSH Faith. | Religion--Philosophy. | Knowledge, Theory of (Religion) | Christianity. | Philosophical theology. | Religion--Philosophy. | BISAC RELIGION / Christian Living / Spiritual Growth | RELIGION / Christian Theology / Apologetics
Classification: LCC BR100 .H54 2019| DDC 230.01--dc23

My thanks to Phil Zahreddine, Nathan Snow, and others for helpful comments, and to Reid Satterfield and Sarah Hamaker for helpful edits.

Cover and layout designed by SWH

CONTENTS

ARGUMENTS ABOUT GOD'S EXISTENCE

IMPLICATIONS

POSTSCRIPT

PREFACE

*T*he New Testament pictures Jesus as someone who enters our life, calls us into discipleship, and invites us to participate in kingdom work. In Matthew's Gospel, for example, Jesus finds Peter and Andrew fishing and calls them with these words: *"Follow me, and I will make you fishers of men."* (Matt 4:19) As a rabbi, Jesus offers his lifestyle and teaching as a model to follow, but, unlike other rabbis, Jesus seeks out his students. Their response is remarkable—they drop their nets and follow Jesus (Matt 4:20)—because their simple faith in Jesus amounts to only two things: obedience (responding to Jesus' invitation) and action (following Jesus). Other than obedience and action, they only know that he is a rabbi (Matt 4:17).

This model of simple faith—obedience and action—extends also to us, but how do we know what we know? In this age of suspicion and doubt, this question has particular significance because Jesus' call—*"follow me"*—comes to us second hand. We read an English text translated from Greek that was itself copied by hand for almost two thousand years after the Apostle Matthew wrote it. He wrote it based on the testimony of others, having himself been called later (Matt 9:9), and, then, only after the resurrection made it obvious that these events had eternal significance. The epistemological question—How do we know what we know?—is therefore a reasonable and interesting question worthy of study even in the absence of doubt.

A complete spirituality must answer four questions typically posed in philosophy:

1. Metaphysics—who is God?

2. Anthropology—who are we?

3. Epistemology—how do we know?

4. Ethics—what do we do about it? (Kreeft 2007, 6)

My first two books—*A Christian Guide to Spirituality* and *Life in Tension*—address the metaphysical question, and my third book—*Called Along the Way*—explores the anthropological question in the first person. In this book, I explore the epistemological question writing, not as one with specialized training in philosophy but as one cognizant of the need, both as a Christian and an author interested in Christian spirituality, to have a reasonable answer to the question—How do we know?

In approaching this question, it is easy to get lost in the weeds. It is interesting that Copernicus' observation that the planets revolved around the sun simplified the mathematics of planetary motion, because the earth was not the true center of the solar system.[1] In the same manner, our lives are simplified when we acknowledge that we are God's creation, not the creators of our own universe.

The act of knowing makes us aware of our distance from a holy God, and our own weakness and vulnerability as human beings. Thinking sets us apart from the object of our reflection just like God was set apart from his creation, not part of it.[2] Knowledge is also at the heart of sin, as we learn in Genesis 3 when Satan tempts Eve. Scripture praises knowledge when its object is God, but cautions us when it leads to pride.[3] So we should take the attitude of the Apostle Paul, who vigorously defends the faith and points people to God (2 Cor 10:5–6).

In this writing project, I break the epistemological question into a series of questions:

1. How do we approach information, learning, and making decisions?

2. Who is God?

3. What are the arguments for God's existence?

4. What does all this imply?

This last question may seem out of place in this discussion, but it is, in fact, critical to our evaluation of faith arguments. Faith is a life and death matter because, as human beings, we strive for meaning, cannot face life without it, and feel threatened when our assumptions about faith are questioned. When the Apostle Paul repeats an early Christian confession:

> For I delivered to you as of first importance what I also received: that Christ died for our sins in accordance with the Scriptures, that he was buried, that he was raised on the third day in accordance with the Scriptures, and that he appeared to Cephas, then to the twelve. (1 Cor 15:3–5)

Here he starts by describing it as being *"of first importance"*. He is not writing about a philosophical hobby-horse—he is talking about a faith for which he was later martyred. Faith is both our anchor and our compass. Anything worth dying for is something worth living for.

Soli Deo Gloria

INTRODUCTION

Overview

Our post-Christian, Western society challenges faith, strips life of meaning, and leaves us to sort what we know for ourselves, an epistemological problem. Much like the Great Recession created a need to learn more about personal finance, the postmodern[1] crisis of faith has created a need to learn more about epistemology, the study of how we know what we know.

The need for confidence that what we know is true also arises because life is too short to test every assumption for ourselves. Imagine a world in which we argued about the definitions of red, yellow, and green every time we pulled up to a stoplight? In this ad hoc information age, it is important to examine basic assumptions in our thinking much like it is important to build a house on a solid foundation. Faith is not optional; neither is the epistemological task.

The need for confidence also depends on who we are as human beings. The New Testament teaches that the heart and mind are inseparable. Confidence is not a mind-game; it also depends on our emotional response. This interdependence implies that our epistemology depends on our interpretation of anthropology (theory of humanity).

Anxiety arises when we depend on knowledge that we cannot evaluate for ourselves. Our emotions reflect our assessment of threats to our being, social position, and livelihood. Who could concentrate on studying Einstein's theory of relatively if you worried about the roof collapsing? Living in a complex, technological world where the consensus on basic values has broken down creates anxiety because we can no longer trust that the experts we rely on value our lives more than their own economic interests. This risk of loss increases our interest in the epistemological task.

Being part of a cause greater than ourselves provides security and meaning to life that we cannot attain as individuals. Only once we feel secure can we become creative and begin to explore other things. We care about the grand story of humanity, the meta-narrative, because it defines our role and our boundaries, giving life meaning and a sense of security. Because, as postmoderns, we no longer believe in objective truth that can be distilled easily into simple concepts, we are forced to ask who offers the best story of where we come from, who we are, and where we are headed.

Incentives to Examine Faith

*C*hristians face an enormous challenge in living out their faith today because major tenets of Christian theology are being openly challenged in the media, schools, and the political arena. What are we to believe and, then, how are we to apply those beliefs in our daily decisions?

Epistemology is an intimidating subject normally reserved for those with a strong background in philosophy, but, like it or not, each of us has to answer these questions of faith without the benefit of a doctorate in philosophy. Regardless of our preparation to meet this challenge, three reasons force us to pay attention to epistemology.

The first reason for our interest in epistemology is that the rapid rate of cultural change in this generation is a consequence of a fundamental shift in philosophy. Modernism is dead; postmodernism is unstable and appears to be breaking down into a form of tribalism (Veith 1994, 143–156). Philosophical change directly affects our understanding of theology and how to apply it. The breakdown of the division between church and state makes this change especially obvious because this division has been a fundamental boundary since long before the modern period.[1]

The second reason for our interest in epistemology is that when philosophical transitions occur, institutions leveraged on prior philosophical assumptions must seek new foundations. Modern democracy works well when citizens stay informed and vote based on their own self-interests, but flounders in a premodern traditional or postmodern tribal culture where citizens refuse to stay informed and vote based on their affinities. Evidence of this floundering can be seen when Congress typically cannot reach a consensus and the President or the Supreme Court needs to broker a new consensus. Institutions actively engaged in self-preservation frequently fail in their basic missions and offer little shelter to those dependent on them.

The third reason for our interest in epistemology is that the lost sense of God's transcendence diminishes our own vision. Smith (2001, 1) observes:

> In different ways, the East and the West are going through a single common crisis whose cause is the spiritual condition of the modern world. That condition is characterized by loss—the loss of religious certainties and of transcendence with its larger horizons...The world lost its human dimension and we began to lose control of it.

If God's credibility suffers, then we look for answers to politicians, television personalities, and charlatans of all stripes—idols—

who invariably let us down hard, as the Bible warns all idols do.

This same logic applies to churches and denominations which becomes obvious when, in the name of self-preservation, they deviate substantively from biblical teaching and fail to offer thoughtful and faithful answers to questions that arise. Forced to answer fundamental questions of faith for themselves, individuals often reject faith, leaving one open to unreflective acceptance of pseudo-religious alternatives, atheism, or syncretistic practices. Everyone has a belief system; not everyone is equipped to reflect systematically on what they believe.

Now, some of you may be thinking: *Why do I bother myself? Why can't I just apply scripture and be done with it?*

Of course, you can. However, if you do this on Sunday morning and forget about it on Monday morning, then do you honestly believe your church's teachings or are they simply an interesting mental exercise? Blind acceptance of faith invariably leads to beliefs only tentatively held and of little use when life's challenges arise. Epistemology provides a lens for viewing the current age through the eyes of scripture so that it is more meaningful and easier to apply.

How We Learn

We most frequently follow one of three approaches to learning: the behavioral approach, the rational approach, and the authoritative approach. In the behavior approach, we follow the path of least resistance—we do more of things that have positive reinforcement and less of things with negative reinforcement. In the rational approach, we explore the alternatives presented and chose the best alternative based on our exploration of all available information. In the authoritative approach, we may start with either the behavioral or the rational approach, but we limit our exploration to options suggested by a mentor.

An example of the authoritative approach is found in Luke 8 following the Parable of the Sower, where Jesus gives his disciples a lesson:

> Now the parable is this: The seed is the word of God. The ones along the path are those who have heard; then the devil comes and takes away the word from their hearts, so that they may not believe and be saved. And the ones on the rock are those who, when they hear the word, receive it with joy. But these have no root; they believe for a while, and in time of testing fall away. And as for what fell among the thorns, they are those who hear, but as they go on their way they are choked by the cares and riches and pleasures of life, and their fruit does not mature. As for that

in the good soil, they are those who, hearing the word, hold it fast in an honest and good heart, and bear fruit with patience. (Luke 8:11–15)

In this context, how do we know what we know? In the passage, Jesus gives us an interpretive key: *"The seed is the word of God."* We understand and accept the lesson in this passage for two reasons. First, the key comes from a reliable source: Jesus. As Christians, we trust the Bible to tell us about Jesus who is known to use parables in his teaching. Second, the key itself, like the Copernican mathematics of planetary motion, makes intrinsic sense—the parable which was posed as a riddle suddenly becomes meaningful like a lock opened with a key.

While not all problems that we are confronted with take the form of a riddle unlocked with a key, Jesus' laconic (use of few words) parable demonstrates the value of the authoritative approach in learning. Most learning both inside and outside the church follows the authoritative approach, in part, because it accelerates our learning.

Our discomfort in the present age arises because we have many more choices than tools for selecting among them, and we have been convinced that we should prefer the rational approach, even though even the best scientists rely on the informed opinion of others. Just like good seminary students apprentice themselves to the best pastors and theologians, the best scientists compete to be students in the best universities and with the best professors. It seems to be no accident that Dietrich Bonhoeffer, one of the most influential theologians of the twentieth century, was the son of Germany's finest psychologists of that day.[1] The question as to whether the authoritative approach is a valid approach to learning is moot because everyone uses it.

If we try to avoid the authoritative approach, we actually put ourselves at risk. If we adopt the behavioral approach to every problem, for example, the positive reinforcement of addictive substances and addictive circumstances will lead us to self-destruction. Alternatively, if we adopt a rational approach to every problem, analysis paralysis will lead us into burnout, and untimely decisions will cause us to miss opportunities. In this context, trusting a divine mentor can lead us to limit our choices to better choices.[2]

The Parable of the Sower offers at least one other insight into our learning process. Jesus tells his disciples a story in the form of a parable. Storytelling accomplishes at least three things relevant to the learning process. Stories are:

1. Easily understood and remembered.

2. Suggest insights into how the world works indirectly, which does an end-run around our natural, human

resistance to taking advice.[3]

3. Provide context for the words used in the story, defeating the criticism that the meaning of words depends solely on the social context of the reader.[4]

Far from being unsophisticated, Jesus' use of parables suggests a level of sophistication seldom equaled in the modern and postmodern eras, even in mass media.

Consider what Geisler and Zukeran (2009, 197) refer to as parabolic apologetics—using a story to convey a truth. Characteristics of this method found the Gospel of John include:

1. The use of the story form,

2. The teaching through an indirect approach—the audience affirms the point before realizing they themselves are in focus,

3. The logic is *afortiori*—a truth from everyday life applies also to spiritual matters,

4. The parable uses self-discovery to give the audience a sense of ownership of the message,

5. The parable is sensitive to those caught in sin (Geisler and Zukeran 2009, 188–89).

The Bible pictures God as a god willing to reason with us. "*Come now, let us reason together, says the LORD*" (Isa 1:18). Still, humility requires that God be willing to argue a case, not force one, on reluctant sinners.

Importance of Meta-narrative

A meta-narrative is a grand story that contains and explains our personal stories.[1] The meta-narrative of scripture, for example, is often described as a three-act play: creation, fall, and redemption (e.g., Wolters 2005). Continuing the analogy to the theatrical model, Vanhoozer (2016, 98) argues for five acts:

> Act 1: Creation, the setting for everything that follows (Gen 1–11)
>
> Act 2: Election of Abraham/Israel (Gen 12-Mal)
>
> Act 3: Sending of the Son/Jesus (the Gospels)
>
> Act 4: Sending of the Spirit/Church (Acts—Jude)
>
> Act 5: Return of the King/day of the Lord/consummation/new creation (Rev).

Other authors describe the meta-narrative of scripture in terms of covenants, such as the covenants with Adam, Noah, Abraham, Moses, David, and Jesus, which provide insight into our relationship with God (e.g., Hahn 2009). Each of these frameworks have a slightly different focus, but all serve to offer meaning within the narrative of scripture to the relationship between God and his creation.

The Book of Genesis begins with a picture of a creator God

whose sovereignty rests on the act of creation and who creates us in his image as heirs to this created kingdom. Describing God as creator implies that he transcends creation where transcendence implies standing apart from and sovereign over creation. This act of creation implies love because God allows creation to continue existing after the fall and even promises redemption (Gen 3:15).

This picture of a sovereign God is key to understanding both God's role in our lives and who we are, especially in the postmodern age because God's sovereignty depends on God transcending our personal worlds. When faith is viewed as a private, personal preference rather than acknowledging our place in the meta-narrative of scripture, then all meaning is lost. If God is no longer transcendent, God is also no longer sovereign. As the Apostle Paul writes:

> And if Christ has not been raised [from the dead by a transcendent God], then our preaching is in vain and your faith is in vain. (1 Cor 15:14)

Jesus' resurrection validates God's transcendence; if you do not believe in miracle of resurrection, then scripture is only of historical interest.

But you say—*that's not true; we still worship God and still believe in his sovereignty.*

Yes, but the words are hollow if Sunday morning worship

serves only to jazz us up, but our Monday morning lives differ little from the atheist in the next cubical. If God is not transcendent, then he is also not immanent—not in our thinking, not in our daily lives. A Sunday morning god is no god at all.

Phillips (1997, 7) wrote:

> The trouble with many people today is that they have not found a God big enough for modern needs. While their experience of life has grown in a score of directions, and their mental horizons have been expanded to the point of bewilderment by world events and by scientific discoveries, their ideas of God have remained largely static. It is obviously impossible for an adult to worship the conception of God that exists in the mind of a child of Sunday-school age, unless he is prepared to deny his own experience of life.

While public ridicule of faith was common in the modern age,[2] in the postmodern age our modern institutions have simply begun to crumble as Christian presuppositions have been removed.[3] Smith (2001, 48) observes: *"Today we do not live under a sacred canopy; it is marketing that forms the backdrop of our culture."* Modern institutions, such as the mega church, public schools, democracy, corporations, and professions, presume objective truth, personal discipline, integrity, and human rights—all products of the Christian meta-narrative that function poorly, if at all, in the absence of that narrative.

As Bonhoeffer (1997, 163) observes:

> The right to live is a matter of the essence and not
> of any values. In the sight of God there is no life
> that is not worth living; for life itself is valued by
> God.

Secular values are a poor substitute for a Christian character because they are lightly held, not deeply ingrained—they are like a house built on a flood-plain with a foundation of sand (Matt 7:24–29).

Think about the modern corporation. Chandler (2002, 1) writes:

> Modern business enterprise is easily defined. …it
> has two specific characteristics: it contains many
> distinct operating units and it is managed by a
> hierarchy of salaried executives.

How could operating units function if employees refused to show up on time? How could managers manage other managers without a basic level of trust? No middle managers existed before 1840 because the first modern corporations were railroad companies organized in the 1850s (Chandler 2002, 3, 81–82). In other words, the modern corporation is a product of the modern era when the belief in objective truth allowed professional managers to evolve.

In this sense, the postmodern age is in the middle of a

transition when our culture no longer looks to our past to find meaning and a new age has yet to emerge on the horizon, giving our lives an end-time feel. To use an Old Testament analogy, we find ourselves wandering in the desert having left Egypt, but not yet having entered the Promised Land (Bridges 2003, 43). The Good News is that the desert is where the people of Israel truly came to know, experience, and rely on God (Card 2005, 16).

Challenges to Faith

O ne of the most seductive arguments against belief in God is the idea that faith is optional. While it is important to understand the reasons for faith, the context for disbelief is equally important. Otherwise, we find ourselves debating primarily with ourselves. Does the disbeliever honestly seek to understand or are the arguments for disbelief a smoke screen for obstinance, laziness, self-centeredness, or some other agenda?

Karl Marx and Sigmund Freud gave two of most famous excuses for why many people believe that God does not exist. Marx (1843) commented that:

> Religion is the sigh of the oppressed creature, the heart of a heartless world, and the soul of soulless conditions. It is the opium of the people.

By contrast, Freud (1961, 30) characterized religion as an illusion, a kind of wish fulfillment. While both Marx and Freud are considered authority figures, the thrust of their argument is not due to a lengthy scientific analysis, but is presented more as simple slander, acceptable primarily as an excuse for decisions reached for other reasons.[1] In a context of a rational decision process, simple slander does not warrant further investigation because the burden of proof lies with those advancing a particular argument to make their case.

Faith undergirds modern science. Knowledge based on the scientific method follows a distinct method for testing knowledge's veracity. These steps are usually employed: a need is felt, a problem is defined, observations are taken, analysis is done, a decision rule is imposed, an action is taken, and responsibility is borne. The first step in the scientific methods (felt need) requires taking assumptions about the current state of knowledge and forming a hypothesis.[2] These assumptions are faith statements for which no testing is normally done.

The key role played in problem definition arose out of research work done after the Second World War. Before the war, American scientists had the best funding and equipment in the world, but their research lagged behind their European colleagues. After the war, American productivity took off with the immigration of European scientists, primarily Jewish refugees. Polanyi's 1962 study of this reversal suggested that these immigrants brought with them the unpublished, indescribable expertise that only the best scientists could muster. In other words, the intuition required to turn a felt need into problem definition proved to be an intangible skill that only master craftsmen,[3] like those making Stradivarius violins, possessed and passed only to their apprentices.

If we treat faith as optional, we undervalue faith and are susceptible to idolatry. The problem of idolatry today has less to do with worshiping statues of pagan gods than with misplaced priorities. We commit idolatry whenever we place anything other than God as the number one priority in our lives. Idoaltry is a sin because it breaks the First Commandment: *"You shall have no other gods before me."* (Exod 20:3). The sin of idolatry is often taken lightly, but this a mistake because idolatry is life threatening.

If the threat of idolatry is not obvious, consider what happens when alternatives to God become our first priority. Common today, for example, is to place work as the number one priority in our life. What happens when we lose our job or our ability to work? Americans, particularly men, are prone to depression and suicide when a job is lost.[4] People who cannot work, like the mentally disabled, the young, the old, the uneducated, are treated badly. When we neglect our faith in God, we end up committing idolatry, which threatens our self-esteem and our relationship with people we should care for.

For the most part, postmodern critiques of Christianity offer criticism without providing an equally wholistic alternative worldview or lobby for rights, but not responsibilities for their particular client groups. Either position is morally reprehensible because they leave many people hopeless and abandoned. Yet, powerful groups have advanced such changes primarily to enrich themselves at the expense of others.[5]

It is illegal to advertise tobacco or alcohol products to minors, but what is the effect of promoting hedonistic lifestyles hourly to adults on national television and every other form of media? Or what about pharmaceutical companies that sell expensive AIDS medications[6] while seeking to expand their markets through lobbying efforts in the media and halls of Congress to promote alternative lifestyles? (Kaufman 2017) Or what about the cynical businesses and churches that simply cater to upscale demographics, regardless of implications? (Wallace 2015) Moral failure is nothing new, but the institutionalization of such failures today is unprecedented and clearly not an accident.

These challenges to faith are repeated daily in the media, in our schools, and in society, yet they lack merit as an alternative to faith and cause significant harm to many people through their promotion of idolatry and other sins that isolate people from God, from themselves, and even from the science that has brought humanity numerous benefits. Many of these challenges to faith either promote or allege deviations from proper mental function making it important to be aware of and mitigate such impacts.

As Christians, we have inherited a worldview that is quite capable of interpreting the world as we know it. In fact, Western civilization is built on premises advanced from the Christian worldview. The question for those who advance criticism of that worldview, normally by picking on some of its assumptions (or disputing its ethical requirements), is not how can we accept those assumptions. Rather, because those assumptions form a coherence and ethically defensible system, the question is whether an alternative assumption can be used to construct a better system.

Why We Care About Epistemology

O ur concern with epistemology is simple: faith is a lifesaver whose absence can cause great suffering.

Viktor Frankl offers interesting insights into faith and the meaning of life. In his book, *Man's Search for Meaning*, Frankl shares both his concentration camp experiences during the Holocaust and his observations as a logotherapist (meaning therapist), observing:

> Every age has its own collective neurosis, and every age needs its own psychotherapy to cope with it. The existential vacuum which is the mass neurosis of the present time can be described as a private and personal form of nihilism; for nihilism can be defined as a contention that being has no meaning. (Frankl 2008, 31)

He defines neurosis as an *"excessive and irrational anxiety or obsession,"* while an existential vacuum (lack of meaning in life) *"manifests itself mainly in a state of boredom,"* which afflicts a quarter of European students and about two-thirds of American students, according to Frankl's own statistics. He concludes that meaning comes not from looking inside one's self, but from transcending one's self (Frankl 2009, 110, 131). In his book, he repeatedly associates this existential vacuum with despair and suicide, based on his experience both as a concentration camp survivor and a professional psychiatrist.

If our culture obsesses about individual freedoms, encourages individuals to look within themselves for meaning, and rejects faith out of hand,[1] then Frankl suggests that we should observe epidemic levels of anxiety, depression, and suicide, as we observe. Lucado (2009, 5) puts it most succinctly: *"ordinary children today are more fearful than psychiatric patients were in the 1950s."* Frankl and Lucado's observations about the emotional state of a society are hard to quantify in a statistical sense, but the *New York Times* recently reported that suicide rates in the United States had reached a thirty year high.[2]

How did we reach this point?

Part of this story is one of a stagnant economy where about half of all Americans have seen no increase in real income since about 1980 (e.g., Desilver 2018). Families under economic pressure increasingly have both spouses working full time, which implies both smaller families and fewer economic and emotional reserves, especially for those with only a college degree or less. When both spouses work, it is harder to set aside Sundays for family and church, reducing spiritual reserves. When a crisis emerges for families already stretched to the limit, the absence of reserves—economic, emotional, and spiritual—can be stressful.

Remove faith from this mix, and the absence of reserves can be devastating. Faith is more than a spiritual reserve, but it is certainly no less.

In reality, faith is primal. Our faith informs our work ethic and our devotion to marriage, which implies it is logically a precondition for economic and emotional vitality. Attacks on our faith are the most basic threats to our life both here and now, and eternally. So we should care about epistemology because our lives depend on maintaining our faith.

Limits to a Cognitive Approach

$\mathcal{E}$ pistemology asks how we know what we know and as- sumes a cognitive approach to learning. The presumption is that human beings are essentially rational and that faith itself is a rational undertaking. The Bible suggests, however, that this cognitive approach has two important limitations when we dis- cuss faith.

Creation Influences Thought

The first limitation arises because we are created, male and female, in the image of a triune God. Being created to live and reproduce in families implies that we experience the world in community. Much as we want our independence, our thoughts, feelings, and language are not entirely our own.

Being created in the image of a triune God reinforces a focus on community. The Bible portrays God as Father, Son, and Holy Spirit—a complete community in the godhead, as Jesus references after the Last Super:

> But when the Helper comes, whom I will send
> to you from the Father, the Spirit of truth, who
> proceeds from the Father, he will bear witness
> about me. (John 15:26)

In imaging a triune God, we image a community, something we can neither fully embody nor understand. By contrast, a unitary god is fixed, stable, and offers mostly an opportunity for self-projection, while a triune God is dynamic, engaging, and alive.

In particular, the language we speak shapes our perceptions of reality in fundamental ways, not the least of which is that it reflects the culture we live and worship in. Our attitudes about gender, work, faith, and many other things are embedded in the words that we use and do not use. We are not alone in this world. Even in our own thoughts and feelings we carry our community with us wherever we go.

The Hebrew Heart

The second limitation of the cognitive approach arises out of who we are. The Hebrew mindset assumed in the New Testament saw mind and body as different parts of a unified whole, whose center is the heart, while the Greeks distinguished mind and body as separate. Confusion arises when we assume incorrectly that the New Testament sees the heart as a body part, and we treat heart and mind as separated, like the Greeks and most secular people.

This confusion implies that the cognitive approach cannot fully inform our faith because it is based on faulty Greek anthropology. As theologian James K.A. Smith (2016, 2) writes:

> Jesus is a teacher who doesn't inform our intellect but forms our very loves…His teaching doesn't just touch the calm, cool, collected space of reflection

and contemplation, he is a teacher who invades the heated, passionate regions of the heart. He is the Word who penetrates even dividing the soul and spirit; he judges the thoughts and attitudes of the heart (Heb 4:12).

Inherent in this statement is the Hebrew view of anthropology cited above—note the two references to heart. What Greek would talk about *"the thoughts and attitudes of the heart"*? Drawing attention to this anthropology, Smith (2016, 5) asks: *"Do you ever experience a gap between what you know and what you do?"* If he had the rational mind in view, no such gap would exist but, of course, we all experience this gap.

This line of thought leads Smith (2016, 7) to observe: *"what if you are defined not by what you know [the mind] but by what you desire? [the heart]"* If our desires are reflected more in our actions than in our words, then this Hebrew anthropology leads us immediately into an inconvenient, but vital, discussion of ethics because our hearts are not lily-white clean as our words. It also forces us to discuss how we know what we know (the epistemology question), because our hearts are not so easily persuaded to follow even our own thoughts. Suddenly, much of the New Testament language sounds less churchy and more informed by an alternative world view, one decidedly not Greek.

Clearly, we cannot talk about thinking independent

of feelings, and we cannot think entirely independent of the communities that we reside and worship in. We need to proceed to treat them as interdependent, complicated as that might be. Still, as best we can, we need to understand better how we know what we know before we can even talk about our faith.

USES AND ABUSES OF INFORMATION

Overview

*A*s discussed in the introduction, the scientific method hangs critically on the skill and intuition with which felt needs are transformed into problem definitions. The assumptions used in this intuitive process work essentially the same way as faith informs our daily life.

The language we speak shapes our perceptions of reality in fundamental ways, not the least of which is that it reflects the culture in which we live and worship. Our attitudes about gender, work, faith, and many other things are embedded in the words that we use and do not use. We are not alone in this world even in our own thoughts and feelings—we carry our community with us wherever we go.

In this chapter, I examine the uses and abuses of information in our thought processes. As I discuss issues affecting us as individuals, note how individual and community effects often mirror one another, as the case of rumination highlights.

Positivistic and Normative Information

*D*uring the modern period, objective truth was believed to be knowable and characterized by the distinction between positivistic and normative information. Johnson (1986, 16, 18) writes: *"Positivistic knowledge is synthetic knowledge that deals with the characteristics of conditions, situations, or things in the real world."* Meanwhile, he defines normative knowledge as: *"Prescriptive knowledge as well as knowledge about values—about goodness and badness."*

The usefulness of this distinction between facts and values arises when people disagree primarily on details, not deeply held values. An old saw goes that we are each entitled to our own opinions (statements of values), but not our own set of facts (statements about what is). In the postmodern era the consensus on basic values has broken down blurring the line between facts and values.

Starting Point for Science

If the consensus on basic beliefs has broken down, then what exactly were the beliefs that brought us the modern era, science, and business?

Some of the earliest work on this question was done by German sociologist Max Weber, who wrote *The Protestant Ethic* and the Spirit of Capitalism (1930). Griswold (1934, 475–476) summarized Weber's argument:

> Calvinism released the business man from the clutches of the priest, and sprinkled holy water on economic success. According to him {Weber]. John Calvin defend the taking of interest on loads, which the medieval church had condemned under the name of usury.

While the usury prohibitions are no doubt important, the bigger picture is that over the past century analysts have recognized the link between religious views and modern institutional development.

Going into the nineteenth century, nearly everyone in Western countries subscribed to belief in one God who created the heavens and the earth (Gen 1:1), as expressed in the Shema: "Hear, O Israel: The LORD our God, the LORD is one." (Deut 6:4) It is not surprising that in the early years of the modern era, the best scientists (e.g., Newton, Galileo) were often religious individuals, Jews and Christians, influenced not only by their intellect, but by their faith in one benevolent God.

Other belief systems do not offer this same support for scientific investigation. If more than one god were believed to exist, as with polytheism, then this unity of principles would seem arbitrary, and one would not spend a lot of time and effort to pursue such an idea. Why wouldn't another set of principles exist in the realm of another god?

Likewise, if all of nature were considered sacred, as pantheists believe, scientific investigation might be considered sacrilegious, something not worthy of institutional support.

Consequently, the unity-of-God principle in Judaism and Christianity proved important to the growth of science because one creator implies one set of scientific principles applied to the entire universe. While this unity-of-God characteristic is also shared with Islam, the openness of Islam to scientific inquiry has historically been spotty.

Breakdown in the Modern Consensus

If the truth of a statement is a composite of fact and value, then the breakdown of consensus about values leads to doubts about objective truth. For example, a deconstructionist (someone who questions all authorities and focuses on power relationships) might argue that facts depend on whose value system is imposed.

One example of how religious values might affect other values arises in the attitude about keeping pigs. When the Gospel of Matthew writes: *"Now a herd of many pigs was feeding at some distance from them."* (Matt 8:30) The implication here is that this region is outside the Jewish Nation of Israel; it may also infer that the people in this region are gentile and, perhaps, morally corrupt from a Jewish perspective.

This interpretative gloss suggests that the observation of pig ownership and the inference of moral corruption can blur the distinction between fact and value as assumptions about religious views change. Christians usually eat pork while Jews, Muslims, and vegetarians typically do not.

One might observe that a farmer owned one hundred pigs (a statement of fact) while the value of those pigs might depend on whether your religion accepts pork as a food item (a value statement). In a country where pork consumption is not accepted, pig ownership might even be provocative.

Effect on Professionals

The breakdown in consensus about basic values not only makes conversation about disputable matters more difficult, it also challenges authority figures, such as professionals. One forgets that professionals are specialists whose experience focuses on making fine distinctions that might not be meaningful to an ordinary person. When deeply held values are in flux, small values get less attention, and making such distinction adds less value outside a strong business environment. Thus, we see that some professionals (e.g., doctors, lawyers, engineers) continue to

earn high incomes, but more generally the status of professionals
and craft focus has declined.

Foundations for Faith and Life

*F*aith is indispensable in perceiving our world, what we consider good and bad, what we invest time and energy in learning more about, and how we make decisions, as discussed earlier. As with mathematical reasoning, faith provides the assumptions on which we base our analyses.

Our Rock

One of the most fundamental defenses for faith cited in the Bible arises in a parable told by Jesus:

> Everyone then who hears these words of mine and does them will be like a wise man who built his house on the rock. And the rain fell, and the floods came, and the winds blew and beat on that house, but it did not fall, because it had been founded on the rock. And everyone who hears these words of mine and does not do them will be like a foolish man who built his house on the sand. And the rain fell, and the floods came, and the winds blew and beat against that house, and it fell, and great was the fall of it. (Matt 7:24–27)

Jesus might easily have addressed a room full of mathematicians because the order and stability of the created universe testifies to God's existence and sovereignty.

Kurt Gödel (1931), a Czech mathematician, who was born in 1906, educated in Vienna, and taught at Princeton University, is famous for his *Incompleteness Theorem*. This theorem states that stability in any closed, logical system requires that at least one assumption be taken from outside that system. If creation is a closed, logical system (as having only one set of physical laws suggests that it is) and exhibits stability, then it too must contain at least one external assumption (Smith 2001, 89).[1] This is why computers cannot program themselves and why depressed people are advised to get out of the house and do something outside their normal routine.

As creator, God himself fulfills the assumption of the *Incompleteness Theorem* (Smith 2001, 89) not only for us as individuals, but for the universe itself. Most eastern religions fail to grasp the significance of the creation account—*"In the beginning, God created the heavens and the earth."* (Gen 1:1) How can there be an alternative path up the mountain to a Holy God who stands outside of time and space because he created them? Obviously, there is no other path up the mountain because as sinful people we are bound by time and space—we cannot approach a holy god. Humans have tried to build towers up to God since the Tower of Babel (Gen 11:1–6)

God must come down the mountain because we cannot go up it. As Christians, we believe that God came down to us in the person of Jesus Christ, a point reiterated on the Day of

Pentecost with the giving of the Holy Spirit.

Divine Mentor

God's transcendence makes Christ's immanence foundational for our faith. The idea that God takes the further step through the Holy Spirit to become active in our lives is even more remarkable.

The Prophet Isaiah was the first to describe the long-anticipated Messiah as a counselor (Isa 9:6), much like Jesus describes the work of the Holy Spirit:

> But the Helper, the Holy Spirit, whom the Father will send in my name, he will teach you all things and bring to your remembrance all that I have said to you. (John 14:26)

What is most interesting about God's willingness to mentor us is not just that we have the world's most powerful person on our side, but that God mentored us from the beginning, as we read in Genesis:

> Now out of the ground the LORD God had formed every beast of the field and every bird of the heavens and brought them to the man to see what he would call them. And whatever the man called every living creature, that was its name. (Gen 2:19)

The word picture here describes the act of a loving parent. God could have just put Adam and Eve in the Garden of Eden as slave-gardeners or he might have acted like an omnipotent, omnipresent, and omniscient helicopter parent, but instead he gave them responsibilities and spent time with them, like a good mentor.

The Problem of Rumination

For I do not understand my own actions.

For I do not do what I want,

but I do the very thing I hate.

(Rom 7:15)

*W*e are the best fed and most pampered generation of all time, yet, our young people and senior citizens are committing suicide at historically high rates (Tavernise). Why?

One answer is that we have become painfully isolated from ourselves: *"We live in a society in which loneliness has become one of the most painful human wounds"* (Nouwen 2010, 89). Our isolation has been magnified by a loss of faith and community, leaving us vulnerable to anxiety and depression.

Importance of Mental States

Our mental vulnerability affects our ability to make informed decisions about faith or even matters of our own care. Bonhoeffer (1997, 160) observes:

> When a person who suffers from acute depression asks for his life to be ended, ought we then overlook the fact that we are concerns here with a request made by a patient who is not his own master?

What information do we take seriously and what do we reject out of hand? In an environment where objectivity is heavily discounted and the distinction between facts and values breaks down, our ability to sort through information can be seriously impaired.

In outlining proper mental function, Plantinga (2000, xi) defines the concept of warrant:

> Warrant is intimately connected with proper [mental] function. More fully, a belief has warrant just it is produced by cognitive process or faculties that are functioning properly, in a cognitive environment that is propitious for the exercise of cognitive powers, according to a design plan that is successfully aimed at the production of true belief.

He goes on to explain:

> A belief has warrant only if it is produced by cognitive faculties that are functioning properly, subject to no disorder or dysfunction—construed as including absence of impedance as well as pathology. (Plantinga 2000, 153–154)

Because proper mental function is a precondition for warranted faith, those concerned with faith need to care about the mental state of society.

Isolation and Rumination

Isolated people often ruminate about the past. Rumination is: *"...the tendency to repetitively think about the causes, situational factors, and consequences of one's negative emotional experience."* Shebly (2010) In ruminating, obsessing about a personal slight, real or imaged, amplifying small insults into big ones.

For psychiatric patients who are not good at distinguishing reality and illusion, constant internal repetition of even small personal slights is not only amplified, it is also remembered as a separate event. Through this process of amplification and separation, a single spanking at age eight could grow into a memory of daily beatings by age twenty.

Amplified in this way, rumination absorbs the time and energy normally focused on meeting daily challenges and planning for the future. By interfering with normal activities, reflection, and relationships, rumination slows normal emotional and relational development and the ruminator becomes increasingly isolated from themselves, from God, and from those around them.

Technology Mainstreams Rumination

Why do we care? We care because everyone ruminates, and technology leads us to ruminate more than other generations. The ever-present earbuds with music, the television always on, the constant texting, the video game played every waking hour, and the work that we never set aside all function like rumination to keep dreary thoughts from entering our heads.[1] Much like addicts, we are distracted every waking hour from processing normal emotions and we become anxious and annoyed[2] when we are forced to tune into our own lives. Rumination, stress addiction,[3] and other obsessions have become mainstream lifestyles that leave us fearful and lonely even in the company of others.[4]

Tribal Rumination

While this discussion has focused on the problem of rumination in individuals, groups also ruminate. You witness this rumination among cultures that seem to be lost in a time sink. For the American public, we all remember the *"Day that will live in infamy"*—Pearl Harbor Day, December 7, 1941.[5] How many movies and television series have had a theme centered on World War II since then?

The attack on Pearl Harbor motivated the U.S. entry into the war in spite of the fact that the American public had a strong pacifist bent prior to that point. Remembering Pearl Harbor has served since then to remind Americans why they continue to spend enormous sums of money on military preparedness and to fight regional wars around the world that would be hard to justify on the basis of threat to the American homeland.

The recent breakdown of postmodern culture into a kind of tribalism strengthens whenever tribal leaders remind their constituents of past injuries and injustices rather than forging ahead to build a new unity in the wider culture. With the world growing smaller every day because of improvements in transportation and communication systems, even seemingly obscure voices focused on the past can contribute to this devolution of culture through promotion of fear and anxiety.

Faith Mitigates Rumination

Jesus sees our anxiety and offers to relieve it, saying:

> Come to me, all who labor and are heavy laden, and I will give you rest. Take my yoke upon you, and learn from me, for I am gentle and lowly in heart, and you will find rest for your souls. For my yoke is easy, and my burden is light. (Matt 11:28–30)

Self-centered rumination is a heavy burden, not a light one, and Jesus models the Sabbath rest, prayer, and forgiveness that break rumination by encouraging us to look outside ourselves. In Sabbath rest, we look outside ourselves to share in God's peace, to reflect on Christ's forgiveness, and to accept the Holy Spirit's invitation to prayer. In prayer, we commune with God where our wounds can be healed, our strength restored, and our eyes opened to our sin, brokenness, and need for forgiveness. When we sense our need for forgiveness, we also see our need to forgive. In forgiveness, we break the cycle of sin and retaliation in our relationships with others and, by emulating Jesus Christ, we draw closer to God in our faith.

Faith, discipleship, and personal reflection require that we give up obsessing with ourselves. On our own, our obsessions are too strong and we cannot come to faith, grow in our faith, or participate in fruitful ministry. For most people, faith comes through prayer, reading scripture, and involvement in the church, all inspired by the Holy Spirit.

Jesus reframes the world's threats to our identity, self-worth, and personal dignity as promises that we will receive the kingdom of heaven, be comforted, and inherit the earth. But, Jesus makes these promises to disciples, not spectators.[6] These threats to our identity interfere with our spiritual development directly, but they also interfere indirectly by impeding our normal thinking, learning, and decision-making. In many ways, psychiatric dysfunction increasingly has been mainstreamed as gender confusion and drug use have been normalized, celebrities share their addictions with the world, and promiscuity is open and unshamed.

Authenticity

What exactly is beauty and why do we care?

Recently, my kids took me to see a film in which one of Hollywood's most beautiful actresses portrayed a low-class, manipulative, promiscuous woman. The film's plot seemed shallow and pornographic, designed more to offend than to enlighten. I left the theater upset and annoyed, not entirely understanding why.

In his book, *Visual Faith*, William Dyrness (2001, 81) writes:

> Our modern images feature surface and finish; Old Testament images present structure and character. Modern images are narrow and restrictive; theirs were broad and inclusive…For us beauty is primarily visual; their idea of beauty included sensations of light, color, sound, smell, and even taste.

As the old adage goes, beauty is more than skin deep. When it is only skin deep, we take offense, as during my recent trip to the theater.

Beauty More than Skin Deep

In clinical pastoral education, we were taught to look for dissidence between words and the body language of patients that we visited. This disharmony between words and body language is, of course, a measure of truth. In like manner, the Bible paradigm of beauty is that the truth of an object matches its appearance.

Dyrness (2001, 80) writes: "*The biblical language for beauty reveals that beauty is connected both to God's presence and activity and to the order that God has given to creation.*" The human spirit, although undefinable, is obvious by its absence. A beautiful, living human body emptied of its spirit is no more than a repulsive corpse. Morality works much the same way: "*Like a gold ring in a pig's snout is a beautiful woman without discretion*" (Prov 11:22). In biblical use, beauty is almost indistinguishable from the modern concept of authenticity. In both concepts, structure and character complement one another. The surface appearance reflects a harmony within. The beauty we observe in nature reflects fingerprints of our divine creator.

Measure of Truth

Authenticity provides an interesting measure of truth. The gap between form and substance can be subtle, requiring deep discernment. A brilliant sermon can signal inner emptiness while a gold watch without tarnish may signal the substitution of gold plating for gold. Authenticity is a kind of Archimedes principle,[1] a measure of the volume versus density of an idea, person, or piece of art.

Like the less-than-perfect sermon, authentic communication is frequently less perfect than other communication. Because of original sin, we intuit every human being to have flaws. Flawless communication appears too good to be true because it masks our underlying humanity.

Biblical Authenticity

The call for authenticity begins in the third verse of the Bible: *"And God said, Let there be light, and there was light."* (Gen 1:3) Unlike our proclivity to sin as revealed in our flaws, God's words (Let there be light) and actions (and there was light) are in perfect harmony. The contrast between heaven and earth could not be greater. Unlike heaven, which Revelation reminds us needs no light other than God (Rev 21:23), earth requires illumination that God immediately creates.

God's pre-existence relative to creation is underscored in the name that he gives Moses in the burning bush. אֶהְיֶה אֲשֶׁר אֶהְיֶה (Exod 3:14 WTT) that can be translated either as *"I am that I am"* or *"I will be who I will be."* Or in vernacular English: *"I am the real deal"* that implies authentic being—something original that cannot be wholly copied. By contrast, human beings, created in the image of God, possess only the potential for authentic being because sin gets in the way.

Jesus talked a lot about authenticity and about its inverse—hypocrisy. Perhaps his most famous statement about hypocrisy began with an admonition: *"Judge not, that you be not judged."* (Matt 7:1) We frequently judge people by our own estimate of the degree of their hypocrisy. In a book with an ironic theme of authenticity, Howard Thurman (1996, 106) observed about the woman caught in adultery: [Jesus]

> met the woman where she was, and he treated her as if she were already where she now willed to be. In dealing with her he 'believed' her into the fulfillment of her possibilities.

For Jesus, the tension between our desires and actions measured not just our authenticity, but also our proclivity to sin. Anger leads to murder; lust leads to adultery (Matt 5:22, 28).

God's Easter Eggs

Harmony of form and appearance suggests authenticity. If the beauty we observe in nature reflects God's fingerprints, does this indicate that God is good or are we simply projecting our thoughts on natural landscapes?

From statistics we know that correlation does not indicate causality. A theory is required to suggest why a measured correlation suggests causality rather than random association.[2] If sunspots are associated with weather on earth, what explains this relationship? Authenticity fits into this discussion of causality because the harmony of form and appearance could easily be entirely random—the world could just as easily be an ugly, inhospitable mess, or a humble inkblot (Smith 2001, 205). In fact, in an entirely random world, authenticity could, in fact, be a rare event, making it unlikely to exist in the absence of intentional design (Keller 2016, 226).

God's goodness and superabundance serve as trademarks of his handiwork. The simplicity of mathematics in a complex world likewise appears like another one of God's Easter eggs— scientific discoveries intentionally placed where his children would find them.

Authenticity as Critique

At a dinner party years ago, Ruth Graham learned that an older gentleman sitting next to her was the former head of Scotland Yard, the British equivalent of the U.S. Secret Service. Because part of his responsibilities included dealing with counterfeit money, she remarked that he must have examined many counterfeit bills.

> On the contrary, Mrs. Graham, I spent all of my
> time studying the genuine thing. That way, when
> I saw a counterfeit, I would immediately detect it.
> (Lotz 2000, 3)

When authenticity is present, inauthentic substitutes appear gaudy or cheap, a kind of visual lie.

LEARNING BEHAVIOR

Overview

*A*s discussed earlier, how we learn depends on proper mental function unencumbered by environmental stresses, disorders, disfunction, or pathologies and directly affects the quality of decisions we make. Learning processes are especially important for the community of faith because as Christians we honor all age groups and stages in life.

Under the best of circumstances, learning processes challenge the quality of our decisions. Behavioral learning processes can lead to logical traps, while rational learning processes can be infinitely postponed in the search for more information. In this context, the scientific method can help organize learning processes and improve problem solving. But, moral training and the use of mentors helps avoid logical traps, reducing search costs and increasing learning efficiency.

I present a model of culture that pictures culture as the cumulative deviations from perfect rationality in making decisions. Christian culture is defined similarly as deviations (sin) from perfectly following the example of Christ. While this definition of culture may seem unduly negative, it allows us to understand the critical role of decisions and learning in our cultural development and to maintain a healthy skepticism of the role of culture in our lives.

The World of Perception

O ne of the oldest photographs of me as a baby shows me in a high chair wearing a diaper and a top covered with a bib. I am smiling with my hands in the air and oatmeal on my face. The date on the photograph is February 1954, when I was no more than three months old.

Do I remember this early meal? Hardly. Did I climb into this chair or prepare my own food? Hardly. We know, however, from the picture that I am well fed and cared for because I am plump and happy. We suspect that I have a mom that loves and cares for me, but she is nowhere in the picture.

How does a baby perceive his world?

As parents and siblings, we know that infants need constant watching because everything in arm's reach goes straight into the mouth. Science tells us that babies are actually born blind, but babies can still feel, smell, and hear, albeit the mouth has priority. For the baby, trying something generally means putting it in the mouth. No amount of reasoning by mom will change that behavior.[1]

So how do infant perceptions change with time?

If stuff goes into the mouth that does not belong there, infants cry and cry, but that does immediately mean that it won't go into the mouth a second time. If an infant does not like smashed peas, for example, he might try them a few times before learning to refuse them on sight.

In the same manner, dad and other relatives may initially hold an infant, but pretty soon he will recognize that they are not mom and may get anxious and cry unless mom is in sight and comforting him.

How sophisticated is an infant's decision-making?

Through tasting, an infant learns that he likes some food and does not like other food—and other random, mouth-sized objects. Good food gets a positive response; bad food gets a negative response. This tasting elicits a behavioral response, either positive or negative.

Through sight, an infant eventually learns to compare his food and visitors with his prior experiences and either accepts or rejects them. Although these comparisons come much later than tasting per se, they form the basis of early rational decision making.

What is an infant's template for thinking about God?

In an infant world, mom is the early model of God's immanence because she brings him into the world and cares for him. Dad's role as progenitor and provider is less obvious and serves as an early model of God's transcendence.

How do infants relate to their parents?

Infants have a definite preference for mom because she cares for them and is always present. This preference only changes once trust is established both with mom and with dad.

Behavioral Learning

*I*n my earlier discussion of perceptions, I argued that we learn to respond behaviorally a long time before any rational decisions are made. Behavioral learning starts with a simple idea: repeat activities that bring pleasure and stop activities that bring pain. Psychologists talk about stimulus (pleasure or pain) and response (repeat or stop; Skinner 1972, 15). Behavioral learning requires no memory, reflection, or patience so even simple, one-celled animals can be shown to employ it.

By contrast, rational learning starts with making detailed assessments of patterns of experiences taken from memory or reflection. The decision rule remains similar: activity A brought more pleasure than activity B, so let's do more of activity A. These comparisons require pattern recognition, memory, and patience that is not required in behavioral learning.

Behavioral Traps

This simple distinction between behavioral and rational learning lies at the heart of many ethical controversies, because behavioral learning can lead to logical traps. For example, the fish that grabs every tasty worm is likely to end up the fisherman's dinner. In a study of such traps, Cross and Guyer (1980, 3–4) write:

> The central thesis of this book is that a wide variety
> of recognized social problems can be regarded

from a third view [Not stupidity; not corruption].
Drug use, air pollution, and international conflict
are all instances of what we have called 'social
traps.' Put simply, a social trap is a situation
characterized by multiple but conflicting rewards.
Just as an ordinary trap entices its prey with the
offer of an attractive bait and then punishes it
by capture…'social traps' draw their victims
into certain patterns of behavior with promises
of immediate rewards and then confront them
with [longer term] consequences that the victim
would rather avoid.

Following this line of thinking, the existence of conflicting
patterns of rewards and punishments create ethical dilemmas in
decisions focusing exclusively on behavioral responses.

For example, a series of short-term benefits followed
by long-term costs arises in the case of smoking. The pleasure
of smoking a cigarette poses no immediate health risk, while a
lifetime of smoking can lead to cancer and early death. The short
pleasure of cigarettes leads one into a pattern of addiction that
might not be chosen if the entire pattern came were known with
certainty in advance. Smoking therefore poses an ethical dilemma
because hypothetical future costs must be compared with
tangible present benefits, which poses a problem for impatient
people. More generally, impatient people have problems with
learning surprises.

A learning surprise occurs when long strings of positive

stimuli are followed by negative stimuli (++++++-), or if long strings of negative stimuli are followed by positive stimuli (------+). Cross and Guyer (1980, 4) refer to this problem as a social trap—a situation defined as having multiple but conflicting rewards. Such patterns disrupt behavioral learning and suggest why habits may be a poor guide in making important decisions. Smoking, gambling, drug addiction, and marital cheating have an incentive structure with long strings of positive stimuli followed by negative stimuli (short-term pleasure leads to long-term pain). Higher education, research, and investment decisions have the opposite pattern: a long string of negative stimuli (cash outlays, lost income, and hard work) followed by positive stimuli (increased status, power, and income).[1]

Incentive for Ethical Training

The Book of Proverbs is sometimes criticized for the many instructions focused on young men not to be tempted into promiscuous or adulterous relationships. For example:

> For the commandment is a lamp and the teaching a light, and the reproofs of discipline are the way of life, to preserve you from the evil woman, from the smooth tongue of the adulteress. Do not desire her beauty in your heart, and do not let her capture you with her eyelashes; for the price of a prostitute is only a loaf of bread, but a married woman hunts down a precious life. (Prov 6:23–26)

Here the allure of sexual relations is seen to lead into an unbalanced relationship that can be exploited through blackmail. Short-term benefits are followed by long-term costs, sometimes referred to as a *"honey trap."*[2] The moral teaching, found in the prohibitions of adultery (Exod 20:14; Deut 5:18) and sexual immorality (fornication; 1 Cor 10:8), helps avoid this trap.

The Marshmallow Test

While trap avoidance motivates ethical teaching, teaching self-discipline (a kind of rational learning) has its own benefits. In the early 1960s, Walter Mischel ran an experiment with preschoolers (four-year-olds) focused on delayed gratification. The children were given a choice: you can eat one marshmallow now or, if you wait about twenty minutes, you can have two. Mischel then tracked the performance of the children over time, reporting:

> The more seconds they waited at age four or five, the higher their SAT scores and the better their rated social and cognitive functioning in adolescence. At ages 27–32, those who had waited longer during the Marshmallow Test in preschool had a lower body mass index and a better sense of self-worth, pursued their goals more effectively, and coped adaptively with frustration and stress. (Mischel 2014, 4–5).

The good news in Mischel's research concerned how self-discipline could be taught, thereby avoiding a lifetime of under-achievement.

If self-discipline is important in worldly success, then why do so many people continue to live a hedonistic lifestyle, pursuing only happiness and pleasure? The short answer is that we become addicted to dysfunctional behaviors much like we get addicted to cigarettes—knowledge about the likelihood of cancer and an early death is normally insufficient to giving up cigarettes (Cross and Guyer 1980, 48, 75). Worse, industries have profited and grown from encouraging people to indulge their addictions—why else would bootleggers and drug dealers be so rich and popular?

Problems with behavioral learning motivate us to teach discipline and patience to our kids that open the door to rational learning.

Rational Learning

> *Behold, I have set before you an open door,*
> *which no one is able to shut. I know that you*
> *have but little power, and yet you have kept*
> *my word and have not denied my name.*
>
> *(Rev 3:8)*

*T*he act of knowing brings us closer to a holy God because rational thinking sets us apart from the object of our reflection, just as God was set apart from his creation, not part of it. Pride is at the heart of sin, which is responsible for Satan's fall, and the bait he uses (to be like God) to tempt Eve (Gen 3). That's why they ate from the Tree of the Knowledge of Good and Evil.[1] Of course, not all knowledge is profitable. Scripture praises knowledge when its object is God, but cautions us when it was motivated by pride.[2] So we should take the attitude of the Apostle Paul when he vigorously defended the faith and pointed people to God (2 Cor 10:5–6).

What is Rational Thinking?

Rational thinking starts with making reasonable comparisons and associations. The word *rational* implies that a conclusion comports with reason or logic. Rational thinking is thinking logically where thinking has to do with the work of the mind, which uses logic and experience to judge rightly.

Rational thinking benefits directly from logic, such as mathematics and mathematical relationships. We might argue, for example, that $1+1 = 2$, which simply states that adding one to one makes two. Alternatively, we might argue that $1+1+1 > 2$, which says that one plus one plus one is greater than two. Simple comparisons, like these two equations, make rational thinking extremely powerful in ordering our thinking.

Rational learning, which is based on comparisons, differs from behavioral learning because we stand back from simple responses to stimuli. For example, suppose I am a high school student trying to decide whether to take a full-time job or to enroll in college. From a behavioral learning perspective, the job provides an immediate benefit of earning money, while college enrollment requires an immediate expense for tuition and living expenses. The behaviorist prefers the immediate benefits of employment over the immediate cost of enrollment. From a rational learning perspective, a comparison of the lifetime earnings on the job to the lifetime earnings after completing a college degree yields the opposite decision to enroll in college. While both alternatives involve uncertain outcomes, the behavior learning model focuses on short-term costs and benefits, while the rational learning model employs longer-term costs and benefits.[3]

Role of Faith

Our faith directly affects our attitude about learning, especially our patience in dealing with future events. Think about our attitude about children. When our children are young, they require a lot of expense and attention. Even if they care for you in your senior years, such benefits are far into the future. Considering only the short-term costs and benefits, the behavior learning model suggests that having children is only a present cost,[4] while the rational learning model weighs the current costs against future benefits.

The calculation applies to living out our faith today in view of our future life in Christ. The sacrifice of praise on Sunday and of living a moral life the rest of the week has both present and future benefits, but only a rational evaluation sees beyond the sacrifice. Faith in God's goodness and provision for our needs is also required.

If blind response to stimulation leaves the exclusively behavioral learner at risk of addiction and of missing out of benefits preceded by costs, the exclusively rational learner falls prey to analysis paralysis. The rational learner patiently considers all available options, comparing costs and benefits. We all know Christians who get stuck evaluating all their options in life decisions and fail to integrate the study of scripture with the way they live. Decision closure is frequently a problem for those specialized in rational decision-making.

The Problem of Closure

Where the behavioral decision-maker needs to develop patience in decision-making, the rational decision-maker needs to determine when to stop seeking additional information. When do we have enough information to make a decision?

This is a classic opportunity to pray for God's guidance. Closure becomes a problem when we become too risk-adverse and use God's guidance as an excuse for inaction, especially when scripture already offers clear guidance.

Consider the story of King Saul and his son Jonathan in 1 Samuel 13–14 in their fight with the Philistines. While Saul waited under the pomegranate tree to pray for reinforcements, Jonathan went out with his armor-bearer to engage the Philistines, looking to God for a sign that he had God's blessing. When God's sign came, Jonathan engaged the Philistines alone killing some twenty men. The Philistine army panicked causing so much noise that Saul and his men entered the battle, soundly defeating the entire army (McManus 2002, 12).

Ortberg (2015, 257) sees the opened door is a fitting metaphor for how God invites us to step out in faith and service rather than having us wait for confirmation and comfort, a rational decision closure process. He writes: *"It's an open door. To find out what's on the other side, you'll have to go through."* (Ortberg 2015, 10) This opened door invitation always appears riskier than it really is because we know who offers the invitation and for what purpose.

Ortberg (2015,15) sees *"God's primary will for your life is not the achievements you accrue; it's the person you become."* As God tells Abram: *"I will bless those who bless you, and him who dishonors you I will curse, and in you all the families of the earth shall be blessed."* (Gen 12:3; 9, 35). In offering such blessings, God invites us to decide which doors to go through as part of our sanctification and our decisions form our character and mold our identity (Ortberg 2015, 8, 16).

Analysis Versus Synthesis

*I*t is common for people to say that they plan to analyze an issue, but what do they really mean? Suppose your professor asks you to analyze an author's point of view and review his book. Typically, an analysis involves breaking a big idea into the smaller ideas that together compose the big idea.

Analysis

For example, a book about the history of the United States might be composed of sections describing the period before colonization, the period of colonization, the Revolutionary War period, the presidency of George Washington, and so on. The analysis focuses on American history, but the details break that history up into manageable time periods and special events. In fact, one might say that American history is a synthesis of these smaller units that help to explain what it means to be a country called the United States.

Synthesis

Notice that a synthesis is used to compose an aggregation of these parts, while an analysis takes the whole and breaks it up into the parts (Dewey 1997, 114). It is fair, for example, to describe the Bible as a synthesis of the historical revelation of God to humankind. The best minds of the church undertook this synthesis historically and continue even now to affirm the special character of the stories and books chosen (John 21:25). This is why the Apostle Paul could write to Timothy:

> All Scripture is breathed out by God and profitable for teaching, for reproof, for correction, and for training in righteousness, that the man of God may be complete, equipped for every good work. (2 Tim 3:16–17).

Another example of synthesis in our faith walk arises when we employ an ACTS prayer. The first part (A) of the prayer is adoration (or praise). We adore God for his mercy, compassion, patience, love, and truthfulness (Exod 34:6), attributes rare in the world, but which characterize God. Having praised God, in the second part (C) we confess our sins and ask for forgiveness because we cannot enter God's presence, except for the sacrifice of Jesus Christ on the cross. Confession marks us as believers in Christ—an insight gained from analysis of Romans 10:8–10.[1] Having praised God and confessed our sins, we then move into the third part (T), where we thank God for the many blessings of this life. Then, in the final part (S), we supplicate—an old-fashioned word for ask—God for his help in our lives and the lives of others. In effect, our synthesis in an ACTS prayer is a short statement of our personal theology.

Importance of Clear Thinking

It is helpful to distinguish analysis from synthesis because both are useful, but in different ways, in organizing and presenting our thoughts clearly (Dewey 1997, 114). For example, a sermon is typically a synthesis composed by the pastor, while the listener is engaged in more of an analysis of what is being said. If the pastor rambles a few observations about a particular passage of scripture without preparation, then the congregation may find the observations interesting but not be able to draw any serious conclusions, even if they take notes. By contrast, the same observations preceded by an introduction with a statement of premise, separated by restatement of premise, and followed by a conclusion repeating the premise may be understood by everyone in the room.[2]

Even in an impromptu speech, you talk about one idea for a couple minutes, transition to a second idea, then transition to a series of other ideas. Transitions are hugely important to bringing your audience along with you. One way to transition is a synthesis (this idea is a part of a larger class of ideas, as in cups to dishes) or an analysis (this idea can be broken into subclasses of ideas, as in cups to tea cups), which Sedniev calls linguistic pyramids. Another way to transition is to use associations, as in a table and a donkey are similar in that they both have four legs (Sedniev 2013, 32–35).

David Kinnaman and Gabe Lyons recently underscored the importance of clarity in church preaching and teaching. They write:

> Many Christians worry about secularism taking over, but secularism shouldn't be our greatest concern. In other words, secularism's advance is downstream from anemic Bible engagement and thin theological thinking. (Kinnaman and Lyons 2016, 227).

Because of the Internet, original documents from the time of the Bible and the early church have never been more widely available[3] and the number of competent researchers and pastors has likewise never been greater. So why are so many Christians having trouble applying their faith in everyday situations? Part of the answer is that we need to take ourselves more seriously as researchers and pastors, and communicate our faith clearly.

The Scientific Method and Objective Truth

*T*he scientific method is a learning method that led to many of the discoveries about the physical world that have defined the modern period. Discoveries in agriculture, medicine, and manufacturing have alleviated hunger and poverty, and have extended the life expectancy of the vast majority of people since the early nineteenth century.

These discoveries have so dramatically improved the lives of modern and postmodern people. In 2018 *Scientific American* reported:

> Rapid declines in infant, child, maternal and late-life mortality during the 20th century led to an unprecedented 30-year increase in human life expectancy at birth from the 47 years that it was in developed countries in 1900.

At the heart of these discoveries was the scientific method.

The Scientific Method

The scientific method organizes research into these steps:

1. Felt need

2. Problem definition

3. Observation

4. Analysis

5. Decision

6. Action

7. Responsibility learning.[1]

The researcher forms an hypothesis out of a felt need in the problem definition step. The researcher then proceeds to collect observations about this hypothesis in the second step. In the third step, the researcher analyzes these observations in view of other discoveries. In the final step, the researcher decides whether to accept or reject the hypothesis, takes action, and bears responsibility for that action.

Research typically takes place in collaborative communities of scientists that share common philosophies, training, experiences, and publications. As researchers make new discoveries, they publish their finding so that other researchers can replicate their results. Thus, over time the knowledge of the physical world grows, and is disseminated throughout the scientific community and applied to practical applications in agriculture, industry, and medicine.

Philosophical Underpinnings

For many years, people believed that using the scientific method did not involve philosophical prejudices, but simply revealed facts about our world. This belief, however, came increasingly under scrutiny as researchers began to apply the scientific method especially to the social sciences. For example, Polanyi

(1962, vii) writes:

> I start by rejecting the ideal of scientific detachment. In the exact sciences, this false ideal is perhaps harmless, for it is in fact disregarded there by scientists. But we shall see that it exercises a destructive influence in biology, psychology, and sociology, and falsifies our whole outlook beyond the domain of science...I regard knowing as active comprehension of the things known, an action that requires skill...Such is the personal participation of the knower in all acts of understanding.

Scrutiny gave way to outcry during the Second World War as people learned of German scientists performing inhuman experiments on prisoners in concentration camps, such as learning the minimum nutritional requirements to prevent starvation and cold water survival rates.[2] Once these controversial research projects got public scrutiny, the philosophical and theological contexts of this research started to be questioned.

One such presumption was that discoveries inconsistent with current theories would seamlessly work to motivate new theories and old theories would be incrementally abandoned. Historical research done by Thomas Kuhn (1996, 6) showed that this was not typically true. More typically, these divergent observations sit around not attracting much attention, but periodically a scientific revolution occurs championed by new scientific communities and prior theories get swept away, like buggy whip manufacturers after the introduction of the automobile. The obsolescence of technologies and the higher incomes that they engendered gave rise to the notion that technological progress was irreversible.

Nature of Objective Truth

One particularly important presupposition in the modern period and in the scientific method had to do with the nature of truth. Arising out of the Christian worldview came the assumption that one objective truth exists that we can discover, if we take the time to investigate (Schaefer 2005, 140). This assumption is reasonable in the physical sciences; it is less tenable in the realm of social science, where cultural assumptions often dictate how particular activities are judged. For example, we can all agree on the weight of a particular bucket of sand, but we may not agree on whether to eat pork or whether it is acceptable to charge interest on a loan.

The existence of objective truth may sound like a trivial issue, but it becomes important in determining the status of professionals, such as scientists, doctors, lawyer, economists, and even pastors. If one objective truth exists, then it makes sense to consult the professional responsible for that subject matter.

If truth is socially defined, as is often argued in the postmodern period,[3] then it is less clear which professional to consult or whether a professional is even needed. In the church, for example, who is most suited to preach and teach the Bible in which translation and with how much training? The answer to these questions is hotly debated within the church, in part, because we have come to doubt the existence of objective truth and to treat the Bible, not as authoritative, but an object of *"modern scientific scholarship"* (Veith 1994, 191).

End of Modernism

In the postmodern world that we live in, rational learning and decision-making are still important, but the cynicism surrounding rationality is pervasive, and it affects our attitude about anyone in authority. Think about the expression attributed to Richard Pryor *"It's a black thing, you wouldn't understand."*[4] The idea behind this expression is that the truth of what is said is determined within a particular sub-culture, and the normal lines of authority in the wider society are not fully recognized within the sub-culture.

Prior to the modern period, authority stemmed primarily from wealth and political power in secular society, and the church's authority stemmed from reverence for God. In the modern period in America, authority still stemmed from wealth and political power, but this authority was increasingly tempered by the knowledge-based power of professionals. Respect for God waned as rational thinking led many to question God's existence. In the postmodern period, respect for both God and professionals has waned, leading to the rise of authority based primarily on wealth and political power.[5] In effect, if objective truth and God's existence is questioned, then my truth and my group's truth take center stage.

Another important result of this lack of belief in objective truth is that it undermines, not only professionals, but also respect for democratic and judicial process.[6] On a theoretical level, if objective truth exists, then through debate and argumentation we come closer to understanding this truth, which is embodied in both our democratic and legal systems. If no objective truth is believed to exist, then debate and argumentation are simply a power play—my truth versus your truth—that does not enhance the credibility of the decision reached.

Those believing in social contract theory, which undergirds democracy, argue that one should buy into the decision because it reflects no more than the cost of a well-ordered society, but here the formation of tribes do not consider others outside the tribe as *"free, equal, and rational."* (Shaffer-Landau 2018, 195). Thus, tribalism violates the assumptions required for social control theory to apply.

Teachers, Mentors, Friends, and Family

Listen to advice and accept instruction,
that you may gain wisdom in the future.
(Prov 19:20)

We seldom learn alone. From a young age, we learn to take advice from our teachers, mentors, friends, and family, who guide and instruct us.

Literature Review

The first step in any research project is to consult prior research. Many academic fields of study invent entirely new terminology for what may be an ancient topic. A trivial example arises between sociology and economics where a sociologist will talk about fields designating bundles of relations (Bourdieu and Wacquant 1992, 16) to describe what an economist calls markets defined for substituting commodities (Marshall 1956, 269–275). This problem of new terminology points to the need to consult advisers familiar with prior studies.

Resistance to Mentors

Resistance to consulting others frequently starts with pride, shame, or the desire to take credit for the work. We may be too proud to ask for advice or be ashamed that we are not already experts on the subject. The desire to take credit for an innovation often motivates the keeping of secrets, but it also limits our productivity. A simple word of advice can eliminate many hours of searching and reduce the number of errors committed in the process. Working as a professional researcher, I often discovered a book in the final stages of a project that would have been helpful starting out—something that a good mentor could have pointed to earlier in the project.

Of course, not all advisers can be trusted and ideas are sometimes stolen. These kinds of problems arise because the hardest step in the scientific method is the problem definition, as previously discussed. Working a mathematics problem is always easier the second time. An adviser or a reviewer must be trusted enough to know that they will not steal an idea or, in an administrative context, take over (or kill) your research project. This problem is no different in a personal context where sharing with a friend that you like someone (or have applied for a job) entails the risk that they will realize that your relationship is uncertain, and they could be emboldened to step in and initiate a relationship of their own.

Still, good friends and supportive colleagues will want you to be successful—to do your best work, to advance your career, and to find happiness. Working together and offering helpful advice speeds the learning process and makea life much more interesting, as will be discussed in the next chapter. In fact, I frequently find prayer does exactly the same thing. When I take time to pray, the first thing that frequently happens is that God reminds me of something that I neglected to do—call a family member or take care of some unfinished business. With such insights revealed, I sleep much better.

Cultural Adaptation

*U*p to this point, most of our discussion has focused on individual behavior and learning, but no one is an island—even Robinson Crusoe was never truly alone before he met Friday.[1] We live and participate in the cultures of our families, workplace, and society that influence our thinking and behavior directly through rules, regulations, and law, and indirectly by structuring the presuppositions that we use in all our decision.

What is Culture?

Culture is term taken from sociology that is often described as the sum of a society's traditions, especially as they pertain to literature, the arts, language, and music. A more helpful framework, however, can be built based on decision requirements in a corporate context. Far from irrelevant to spiritual formation, the culture context of work plays a key role in secular formation. The same framework for culture can, by analogy, help interpret personality.

Nobel laureate economist Herbert Simon defined rationality as making a choice among all possible alternatives. Economists more generally hypothesize that the firm strives to maximize its net present value assuming perfect knowledge of all future cash flows. If all decisions are rational and predictable given knowledge about technology and market prices, this theory implies that a firm has no culture (or no cultural effect) because given a set of circumstances every manager would reach the same decision. In other words, no culture exists among robots outside their original software, unless they are programmed to learn in an idiosyncratic manner.

In practice, we observe that decisions are costly, resources are limited, and decisions are frequently made based on rules of thumb and habit. For these reasons, in part, Simon extended the theory of the firm to limit rational behavior—his theory of bounded rationality (Simon 1997, 88). Culture arises because highly rational decisions are costly. Managers ration their time by applying rules of thumb based on previous decisions and known costs and benefits, not perfect information. These rules of thumb plus manager training and experience determine a firm's decision culture. Interestingly, the costlier rational decisions are, the stronger the cultural effect.

Culture is especially sensitive to failures as opposed to successes because they cost more. When an investment succeeds, the investment is returned and a profit is generated, but when an investment fails, the investment is lost and even more losses are possible. Jung (1955, 57) observes:

> But the psychotherapist learns little or nothing from his successes. They mainly confirm him in his mistakes, while his failures, on the other hand, are priceless experiences in that they not only open up the way to a deeper truth, but force him to change his views and methods.

The point is that both individuals and firms need to learn from their mistakes and failures. Healthy organizations promote *"constructive dialogue"* about both project successes and failures (Stanton 2012, 10).

The existence of culture implies that a firm's history is interesting. The time sequence of decisions and their consequences predisposes the organization toward some growth paths and away from others, a concept sometimes described as path-dependence. The personal histories of leaders are important in understanding attitudes about alternatives and the speed at which decisions are made.

Cultural Personality Types

The existence of culture suggests why organizations develop classifiable personalities. Several widely observed types can be described. Criteria describing these types include preferred decision style, key values, primary mode for training, nature of control process, and default transaction-opportunity cost trade-off. A culture articulates key values in terms of where decisions ideally take place.

Three cultural archetypes stand out in society today that compete for dominance: a traditional culture, a modern culture, and a postmodern culture. A fourth type, a dying culture (or culture under stress), is more of a transition phase than a stable culture. At any time, subcultures within society may favor any one of these four types. Competition among these types is influenced by the resources available and other circumstances in the environment beyond immediate control. This suggests that one or the other subculture can rise in dominance, which can also pass back and forth. Progress from one to another is neither inevitable nor expected because circumstances external to the firm dictate the ideal culture.

The Types[2]

A modern culture delegates authority to line managers, whose leadership role is often earned through technical competence, because good decisions require the objective information they produce. A postmodern culture shares decision authority to assure that decisions are equitable. A traditional culture centralizes many decisions to adhere to senior management preferences. Training and control processes reinforce these cultural preferences.

A dying organization is an organization in crisis. A dying organization may start with any cultural affinity but evolves toward traditional culture. This is because crises consist of a rapid series of nonstandard problems that exceed delegations and require senior management input. Cutbacks likewise strengthen the position of senior managers.

The mix of transaction costs and opportunity costs also reflects cultural affinities. Transaction costs rise with the number of people participating in decisions, while opportunity costs (the cost of not choosing the next best alternative) rise as decision alternatives are excluded. The traditional culture has the lowest transaction costs because it considers the fewest options—only senior manager preferences are consulted. The postmodern culture consults the most people, but it is not particularly reflective—only options actively advocated are considered. Transaction costs in the modern culture fall between these two extremes, but the modern culture prefers a review of all options.

Williamson (1981, 1564) sees both organizational costs constrained by market prices. The implication is that cultures evolve to reflect competitive conditions in the markets that firms serve. The dominant culture type may evolve with both market pressures and leadership changes, which may over time lead to overlapping cultural attributes. An office evolving from a modern to a postmodern type, for example, may begin to exhibit more group decision-making, place less emphasis on academic credentials in assignments and promotions, and rely less on peer review of work products. As Alchian (1950) argues, learning process is likely a combination of trial and error, imitation of successful firms, and deliberative planning because uncertainty makes it unlikely that future market conditions can be fully anticipated.

Behavioral Weaknesses Impede Learning

Cultural types describe attributes at a point in time. Changing circumstances, however, force organizations to learn and adapt. Learning behavior is therefore a key measure of risk management performance. We observe behavior problems when incentive structures disrupt normal learning processes, create logical traps, or exacerbate normal organizational inertia.[3]

An organizational culture mirrors its environment because decisions and rules evolve over time to deal with environmental challenges. Rewards of money, power, and status within an organization accrue to leaders that facilitate this evolution. When prior decisions and rules need to change, a conflict arises because those changes may threaten the social position of those leaders.

Consider the case of a firm in a growing business. Suppose the firm starts out as a specialized firm in a competitive market. As it grows and acquires competitors, it takes market prices as given. As market share grows, it eventually becomes the market and can set price. Further growth requires that it diversify into new markets. At each stage in the firm's growth, the rules for success and risks change (Porter 1980, 191–295). If the organizational culture adapts with a lag and a threat grows quickly enough, firm solvency could be threatened before adaptation is complete.

Christian Culture

Although the Christian faith encourages rational decisions, Christian culture should not be confused with any of the cultural types outlined above. Christian culture differs from these types because the objective of Christian culture is conformity to Christ rather than conformity to the rational model. Still, the above cultural types are also evident in a Christian context, as when dominations employ different polities.

The term polity refers to how a denomination or church is governed. A denomination managed by bishops is likely organized with a traditional culture while a church managed through direct voting by the congregation likely has a postmodern culture. Meanwhile, a church managed by elders and professionally trained clergy likely has a modern culture. Each of these polities can operate differently in practice, but the formal structure of the polity clearly shapes the culture of churches and denominations.

Just like no perfectly rational firms exist, Christians cannot obtain perfection in this life—Christ is the standard, our sacred North Pole, and the Holy Spirit guides us. With our compass set on north, we are not easily led into darkness, but focus on the light. Through the inspiration of the Holy Spirit, we normally avoid logical traps and quickly repent when we fall into one. The basic ideal is that in Christ, we have the perfect guidance system even when our lives are not perfect.

DECISION-MAKING

Overview

*D*ecisions and how we make them define an important part of who we are, separating the successful from the unsuccessful, the faithful from the unfaithful, the men and women from the boys and girls. In an ideal world, we would approach important decisions as well-informed adults who understand our own weaknesses and consider carefully the options presented to us, taking time to consult with our mentors, friends, and family, and being free of dysfunctions, like mental illness or drug use (Plantinga 2000, 108–134). Of course, we do not inhabit an ideal world.

In the corporate world, decisions under uncertainty are clearly more difficult and mistakes are inevitable. Learning the proper lessons from mistakes requires a willingness to consider whether the decisions taken were flawed or merely untimely. The typical response of refusing to repeat an activity cuts short the process of assessment and discourages staff from taking responsibility for their role in it. Firing the manager responsible makes matters worse because of the lost experience with what happened and because other staff will be more reluctant to take risks in the future. Healthy organizations promote *"constructive dialogue*" about both project successes and failures (Stanton 2012, 10).

Culture and experience form our presuppositions. Resource constraints and uncertainty imply that presuppositions will necessarily be part of our decision processes. Understanding how these presuppositions affect our decisions can help minimize unfair discrimination.

At a personal level, we need to go through this same deliberative process when problems arise. Confessing our sin and accepting God's forgiveness helps us take responsibility for our problems; accepting Christ as Lord and Savior means that accepting the Holy Spirit as a lifelong mentor (Acts 2:38). Starting on this process at a young age assures the greatest benefit from a life of faith.

Proper Mental Function

> *Whatever is true, whatever is honorable,*
> *whatever is just, whatever is pure,*
> *whatever is lovely, whatever is commendable,*
> *if there is any excellence,*
> *if there is anything worthy of praise,*
> *think1 about these things.*
> *(Phil 4:8)*

*A*s alluded to earlier, many questions about information, learning, and decision processes have a core concern about proper mental function. This is especially true in view of the unity of feelings (heart) and thinking (mind) that we see throughout the New Testament, as when the Apostle Paul writes: *"And the peace of God, which surpasses all understanding, will guard your hearts and your minds in Christ Jesus."* (Phil 4:7)[2] Similar concerns arise in criticism about the reasonableness of faith.

Modern Complaints about Faith

Plantinga (2000, 136–142) observes that atheist philosophers have criticized Christian belief as irrational but not in the sense described above—Nietzsche, for example, referred to Christianity as a slave religion. Freud described Christianity as *"wish-fulfillment"* and as an illusion serving not a rational purpose, but serving psychological purposes. In Marx's description of religion as *"the opium of the people"* suggests more a type of cognitive dysfunction.

Plantinga (2000, 151) concludes:

> when Freud and Marx say that Christian belief or theistic belief or even perhaps religious belief in general is irrational, the basic idea is that belief of this sort is not among the proper deliverances of our rational faculties.

Plantinga (2000, 153–154, 163) accordingly concludes that the real criticism of *"Christian belief, whether true or false, is at any rate without warrant."* Plantinga's strategy in analyzing the atheist complaints accordingly is to discuss what they are not saying—not complaining about evidence, not complaining about rationality in the usual sense, not offering evidence that God does not exist—to eliminate the non-issues. What remains as their complaint is a twist on rationality—actually more of a rant—you must be on drugs or out of your mind—which is not a serious philosophical complaint except for the fact that so many people repeat it.

Plantinga calls this complaint a charge of cognitive dysfunction. More recent critics are even less formal in their criticism. Ganssle (2009, 4) observes that the New Atheists[3] do not bother to validate their hypotheses and maintain a deliberate strategy of innuendo that he describes as a Nietzschean genealogy—a genealogy given not to prove that one's family includes royalty, but to discredit the family (Ganssle 2009, 136–137). This pattern of arguing dysfunction and innuendo makes it important to clarify what proper mental function looks like.

A Model of Mental Function

In outlining a proper mental function, Plantinga (2000, xi) defines:

> warrant is intimately connected with proper [mental] function. More fully, a belief has warrant just it is produced by cognitive process or faculties that are functioning properly, in a cognitive environment that is propitious for the exercise of cognitive powers, according to a design plan that is successfully aimed at the production of true belief.

He goes on to explain:

> a belief has warrant only if it is produced by cognitive faculties that are functioning properly, subject to no disorder or dysfunction—construed as including absence of impedance as well as pathology. (Plantinga 2000, 153–154)

We accordingly care a lot about the mental state of society when in comes to faith, as cited above in Philippians 4:8.

Education and Goodness

In this argument about proper mental function is a hint of the age-old belief that faith and education are related. In developing the discipline of study, we become are more open to truth, including the truth of God and God's goodness. However, discipline is a necessary but insufficient condition for faith. Faith is an act requiring emotions and the mind working together. The mind alone cannot bring about faith.

Rational Thinking and Sin

Implicit in Plantinga's concept of warrant is a preference for rational thinking, much like an economist would argue consumers consider all competing products, features, and prices before making a purchase. Proper time and effort are taken to consider all the facts pertinent to a purchase and assesses these facts independent of other consumers—no mandates from leaders or fads influence the ideal purchasing decision. Obviously, the economist also assumes that the consumer is not high on drugs, not subject to impulses brought about by psychiatric dysfunction, and able to afford the products under consideration.

The point is that Plantinga's model of proper mental function is a common feature in many fields of inquiry. Interestingly, Plantinga cites the Apostle Paul in his rebuttal of atheistic critiques:

> For his invisible attributes, namely, his eternal power and divine nature, have been clearly

perceived, ever since the creation of the world, in the things that have been made. So they are without excuse. (Rom 1:20)

Paul goes on to share what is essentially the God's curse for rejecting salvation under the new covenant in Christ. The curse is that the disbeliever is *"given over to"* (become a slave of) the desires of their own heart which has, of course, been corrupted by original sin. Paul's assessment here is that disbelievers have specifically fallen into the sin of idolatry (Rom 1:22–25).

Sin appears in Paul's argument as a generic mental dysfunction that obscures rational decisions and destroys relationships by cutting us off from other people and from God. Stealing, adultery, lying, and disrespecting our parents all obviously undermine relationships oftentimes for selfish reasons and are irrational in an atmosphere of full-disclosure in a highly interdependent society.

Proper Mental Dysfunction?

Plantinga's model of proper mental function begs the question— what if a culture evolved that, far from supporting and sustaining proper function, made proper function more costly and unlikely? Wouldn't we see more dysfunction, anxiety, and suicide as people found it harder to thrive and survive?

Suboptimal Decision Environment

*D*ecisions in a society focused on youth culture pose a special problem because of the refusal of many to shoulder responsibility for their actions.[1] Even in the absence of external manipulation, youth culture can undermine decision-making out of ignorance, impatience, and unwillingness to rectify obvious dysfunction.

The Designated Adult

Some families and organizations manage to survive in this environment, not by encouraging greater rationality, but by weakly tolerating a few designated adults who tirelessly attempt to hold things together while many others simply party on, a situation known as *"over-functioning"* (Friedman 1985, 210–212). Gilbert (2006, 17) notes that the over-functioning individual usually pairs up with an under-functioning individual to form one functioning person out of two.

In a church context, a pastor may be hired to rescue the congregation from a decline in membership only to find that members refuse to accept the new members that the pastor welcomes into the church. Churches of this sort may go through a series of pastors and eventually close their doors because the members refuse to adapt to and accept the changing demographics of their community. Parents unwilling or unable to practice *"tough love"* may find themselves saddled with caring for children that fail to launch and for grandchildren engendered by the same.

The One-off Solutions

Postmodern culture encourages this behavior by refusing to insist that participants hold an internally consistent set of values and by preferring one-off solutions to problems that arise (Veith 1994, 175–176). Probably the most obvious example of this problem comes up with the American drug culture that arises, in part, as the dark side of the propensity of Americans to place too high a value of an unsustainable work ethic. Schaeffer (2005, 206) observes:

> The work ethic, which had meaning within the Christian framework, now became ugly as the Christian base was removed. Work became an end in itself—with no reason to work and no values to determine what to with the products of one's work.

When attempts to compete in this unsustainable work culture fail, recreational drug use spirals into addiction and destroys any possibility of further advance in one's career. At the heart of the problem is the attempt to live a licentious lifestyle alongside of a career that requires exacting personal discipline.

In this example, recreational drug use[2] is proffered as a one-off solution to the problem of stress. Instead of living a balanced lifestyle with time devoted both to work and self-care, the worker self-medicates and skips the trip to the gym or the family outing. Drug use starts out as the solution to the problem of stress through self-medication, not perceived as a problem in itself. Clinebell (1978, 19) observes:

> Does the person's drinking frequently or continuously interfere with his social relations, his role in the family, his job, his finances, or his health? If so, the chances are that that person is an alcoholic or on the verge of becoming one.

This confusion between problem and solution can lead to addiction, but—more to the point—it began by trying to find a one-off solution to the problem of stress, rather than mitigating the stress itself.

When the usual pattern of problem-solving is to seek a one-off solution, as in looking for a pill to solve our health problem, we are less likely to perceive the spiritual problem that may be behind many of life's challenges. May (1988, 6–7) writes that of all the addicts that he has treated, the ones able to turn their lives around had some kind of spiritual experience.

Technical Versus Adaptive Change

The pattern of one-off solutions to complex problems is the

natural consequence of Greek dualism, which sees mind and body as separated. This belief contrasts with the unity of mind and body taught in the New Testament, inspired by Hebrew thinking. When complex problems required a systematic response—changing who we are rather than what we do— one-off solutions—the popular *"low hanging fruit"*—may only compound or delay a finding a real solution to our problem.

Heifetz and Linsky (2002,14–18) distinguish technical from adaptive challenges. In a technical change, authorities apply current know-how to solve a problem while in an adaptive change people with the problem must learn new ways to solve the problem. A technical change typically requires nothing more than additional budget (or a change in legislation, a kind of symbolic action) while an adaptive change requires an entirely new approach where we must redefine ourselves rather than some process or technology.

Up-tempo White Noise

Every age has had its distractions. The postmodern era stands out because the volume of the background noise has been turned up significantly while the usual institutions for dealing with it— family, church, community—have been seriously weakened.[3] It is now up to the individual to turn off the cell phone, computer, and other media or, alternatively, screen the massive amount of information available for specific information of use in making decisions.

Meanwhile, the pace of life and work has accelerated, rendering this filtering process for the conscientious decision-maker more difficult to the point of overwhelming. Mishel (2013) reports:

> The average worker worked 1,868 hours in 2007, an increase of 181 hours from the 1979 work year of 1,687 hours. This represents an increase of 10.7 percent—the equivalent of every worker working 4.5 additional weeks per year.

These figures do not count intangibles like answering email and cell phone messages at home.

But not everyone steps up to this challenge. The U.S. Center for Disease Control and Prevention recently reported that life expectancy in the United States declined for the third year in a row due to crises involving drug overdoses and suicide (Bernstein 2018).

Presented with an overstimulating environment, many people opt simply to check out, self-medicate, or insulate themselves with white noise—the omnipresent headset, the television always on, or refusing to leave their homes. This latter option functions much like rumination that keeps the individual from reflecting on their daily challenges as they obsess about events in the past, especially past trauma. The individual who ruminates (or employs white noise) essentially refuses to think about current decisions and, as a consequence, frustrates their own maturing process becoming developmentally impaired.[4]

Toxic Decision Environment

The problem of relying on designated adults, rather than aspiring to maturity, and the habit of seeking one-off solutions both undermine the decision environment that many people face in the postmodern era. Technology makes more information available. The competition among professionals and professional requirements have also increased even as standards of living have plateaued or declined. Many people reach the age of consent or of legal maturity well before they are able to function as self-reliant adults, leaving them unable to make good decisions, vulnerable to manipulation, and unable to advance spiritually.

The record number of millennials living at home[5] and of grandparents raising their children's kids point to an immaturity problem, but it also highlights how remote the American Dream has become for many people. As first highlighted by Adams (1941):

> The American Dream is that dream of a land in
> which life should be better and richer and fuller

for everyone, with opportunity for each according to ability or achievement.

For those unable to support themselves, to own a home of their own, and to have a family until middle age, the incentive to live a disciplined lifestyle and work towards those ends can seem illusive and out of reach.

Decisions and Media Manipulation

*I*n the postmodern world, advertisers discourage careful reflection that considers the advice of friends and family. Instead, they encourage us to rush to make decisions based on the latest fad and deny that bad habits are bad, acting like adolescents. The resulting youth culture that dominates postmodern life offers an advertiser's paradise.

Media and Faith

Modern media constantly pressures religious life, which promotes reflection, responsible action, and connection with family. If this pressure is not clear, ask yourself questions like why are most sermons about twenty minutes or where do you go when you get upset? Twenty minutes is about the amount of time remaining in a thirty-minute television show after the time devoted to advertising is subtracted. If you go shopping when you are anxious, then consider what your grandmother might have done—fifty years ago, it was common to go to a chapel and pray on stressful occasions.[1] If someone wanted to pray in a chapel today, the door would likely be locked.

Psychological Basis for Advertising

In his book, *Winning the Story Wars*, Jonah Sacks talks about the contribution of marketing to cultural changes that we have seen.

Borrowing from the work of Joseph Campbell, Sacks describes the purpose of myth (storytelling) is to help us grow up because we yearn for maturation. But mature adults (self-responsible, free agents) threaten marketers, who typically prefer us to remain adolescents suspended in an immature state and dwelling on emotions like greed, vanity, and insecurity—the bottom rung in Abraham Maslow's pyramid of needs.[2] In this immature state, we are encouraged to feel inadequate and incomplete where consumption of product X, Y, Z can presumably make us complete again (Sacks 2012, 85–86).

Inadequacy marketing directly assaults the spirit of most religious teaching, irrespective of theology, because most religions aid our maturation and help us to contribute to society. Hence, the phrase—the dark art of marketing—is truly dark because the advertiser works explicitly to undermine rational decision processes, stroke anxieties, and tell us stories that sell their products at the expense of undermining our own self-worth (Sachs 2012, 89).

Broken Record Argumentation

In the days before CDs and online music streaming, people bought long-playing records (LPs) that, if scratched, could get stuck in an infinite loop playing the same line of music over and over. This broken-record repetition annoyed greatly the listener and would not stop until you forced the needle to advance or got rid of the broken record.

Advertisers routinely entertain us with unconscious and voluminous repetition—broken-record argumentation—until it becomes the air that we breathe, shaping our perceptions, and leaving us impatient for new and catchy phrases, tunes, and images. By the time our children reach the age of 17, they have spent 63,000 hours exposed to media, 11,000 hours in school, 2,000 hours with their parents, and only 800 hours in church (Baer and Boone 2007, 88).

As parents, pastors, and teachers, postmodern culture outguns us on daily basis, unless we take deliberate steps to focus on the learning process and how decisions ideally get made.

Decisions Under Uncertainty

Decisions that we make are often assumed to be made in a context of certainty about circumstances and outcomes. We use language like, *if I do A, then B will follow*, as if we knew the outcome with absolute certainty. This is an unrealistic assumption, but we assume it anyway to keep things simple.

Why Do We Assume Certainty?

Part of the reason for this simplistic assumption is that decision-making creates anxiety. In clinical trials, Wemm and Wulfert (2017, 1) report:

> Stress connotes events that the individual finds physically, physiologically or emotionally challenging...Prolonged exposure to stress can produce chronically elevated stress levels that cause wear and tear on immune functioning and various physiological systems. In addition, stress also affects cognitive function.

The future is never known for sure and important decisions can affect outcomes, our state of mind, and how others view our competency. Our anxiety levels go down when we are confident of our ability to understand our circumstances and to make decisions.

Experience with Decision Making

In my own experience, my decision skills improved greatly

after I learned to trade commodities, stocks, and options. In trading, procrastinating in decisions proved costly because buying opportunities quickly disappear in a competitive market, which places a premium on prompt gathering and analysis of information. I learned how to limit the markets that I traded, assess information quickly, and to cut my losses when the market did not perform as expected.

Cutting one's losses quickly is important in other contexts. Suppose that I worked in a particular field for a number of years only to find that my chosen field was no longer hot. If I continued to work in that field and to deny the lack of interest of my employers, my career would suffer even if I retained my position.[1] Alternatively, suppose that I reached retirement age and no longer needed in a stressful job to work to earn a living. If I continued to work anyway because the money was good, then I could end up with unnecessary health problems and missed retirement opportunities, like volunteering, writing a memoir, or spending time with grandchildren.

Uncertainty Affects All Aspects of Decisions

Going back to our original example of a decision—if A, then B—we have at least three sources of uncertainty in this simple equation.

First, what if condition A is only partially met or if we mistake our ability to trigger this condition? If I want to purchase a car, I need to have the money necessary for the purchase. What if I do not have the cash and do not know if a lender to make me a loan?

Second, what if the relationship between A and B changes? Suppose I raise the money to buy the car, but it is no longer available for sale?

Third, what if I raise the money for my car and it is still available for sale, but the dealer package does not include the features that I really wanted, like perhaps a car radio, guidance system, or air conditioning, at the price originally quoted?

The point is that uncertainty is common to most circumstances and decisions.

Uncertainty with Investment Decisions

While buying a car can raise a number of issues in itself, the uncertainty level rises when the car is an investment that needs to be paid for out of future earnings. If I work as a traveling salesman, what features in a new car will best enhance my sales performance and ability to repay my loan? The answer to this question depends on future circumstances that I have no control over.

The same problem arises in making decisions about education. In college, when I decided to study economics, I had no idea what an economist could expect to earn and whether studying economics posed a profitable investment decision, but I knew that my father had studied economics and was able to earn a living. I took it on faith that if I followed my father into the economics profession, I would earn a similar income and be able to support a family. In a formal sense, however, I did not make a rational decision based on current expected earnings in the economics profession.

Traditional Versus Postmodern Ethos

One can argue that a defining characteristic of the postmodern era is uncertainty, captured in the popular expression: *"The only constant is change."*[2] This uncertainty is compounded by a lack of consensus on basic values and the rapid pace of changes in technology and social conventions.

Postmodern uncertainty is also in sharp contrast with the stability of traditional society where tradition informs every important decision in one's life—what gender roles we follow, who our friends are, who we marry, what profession we take up, and who and how we worship. Life has meaning in a traditional society because when we accept this guidance, we are rewarded with status and honor.

Postmodern culture questions tradition and focuses on the individual who is responsible for every imaginable decision with little or no guidance. If we succeed as postmodern individuals, we are fully employed, have a medical plan, and can buy stuff, but we have no guarantee of status and honor because the culture's standards keep morphing. Thus, anxiety has become a defining characteristic of the postmodern era.

Assurance of Salvation

Eternal life is the foundation of our serenity as Christians. Jesus tells us:

> My sheep hear my voice, and I know them, and they follow me. I give them eternal life, and they will never perish, and no one will snatch them out of my hand. My Father, who has given them to me, is greater than all, and no one is able to snatch them out of the Father's hand. I and the Father are one. (John 10:27–30)

In effect, Jesus offers peace where the world offers chaos (John 14:27).

The church responds to the postmodern dilemma primarily by emphasizing the assurance of salvation in Christ and, in effect, denial of any form of uncertainty. While Jesus offers peace, he also acknowledges uncertainty and doubt. Listen to the words of Jesus spoken to the father of a boy possessed by an evil spirit:

> But if you can do anything, have compassion on us and help us. And Jesus said to him, If you can! All things are possible for one who believes. Immediately the father of the child cried out and said, I believe; help my unbelief! (Mark 9:22–24)

The father recognizes that his faith is not sufficient for healing; Jesus accepts his prayer and heals the child notwithstanding.

God's mercy through Christ assures us of salvation that we do not have to earn and we cannot be snatched from his hand (John 10:28).

Experience and Presuppositions

From the fourth century before Christ, philosophers have distinguished experience (Aristotle) from theory (Plato). Experience has the characteristic of being concrete and personal, while theory, often the form of classifications, transcends individual experience to distinguish relationships and general trends. Decisions typically focus on new information and take experience and theories as unconscious presuppositions.

Personality Types

Personality types can be classified based on the distinctions made in the process of reflection. Jung (1955, 89–91) distinguished introvert from extrovert, sensation from intuition, thinking from feeling, and judging from perceiving. Using these distinctions to classify an individual's preferred reflective tendencies, sixteen different personality types can be identified.

One can develop hypotheses about how that each of these types would learn and respond to particular challenges. Myers and Myers (1995, 149) write:

> The five types that favored the stable and secure future were all sensing types. The warmest of the sensing types, ESFJ, characteristically favored service to others. Seven of the eight intuitive types favored either the opportunity to use their special abilities or the change to be creative.

Personality types are not predictive in a deterministic sense because people change their classification preferences over time, but they indicate tendency or probability.

While individuals often prefer one or the other yielding classified personality traits, our experiences are shaped by the theories that we hold, and these theories may even permeate our language. An Inuit (Eskimo) language may, for example, distinguish dozens of kinds of ice and snow,[1] while the Zulu (African) language might make no such distinctions, having fewer opportunities to experience ice and snow.

Presuppositions Matter

Plato took interest in this influence of theory on language and asked the question: How do we perceive the idea of a horse? If you had never seen a horse, how would you describe one?[2] In the Bible, one of the first things that God did with Adam was to create new creatures and show them to Adam to see what he would name them (Gen 2:19). Naming is often interpreted in the Bible to indicate authority or sovereignty over the items being named,[3] but it also provides form—the idea of a horse or prior experiences with horses—to our language and experiences. In a broader sense, culture shapes our language and thinking the same way, providing form to outline and bear our experiences.

Example of Police Shootings

Philosophers call this idea of culture providing form to our language and thoughts a presupposition. Presuppositions can take the form of cultural assumptions, even racial stereo-types.

In recent months, presuppositions have been controversial in the context of police shootings where in ambiguous and threatening situations, police are more likely to shoot suspects from one racial group than another, even when they themselves come from the same racial group.

Payne (2006) writes:

> Race stereotypes can lead people to claim to see a weapon where there is none. Split-second decisions magnify the bias by limiting people's ability to control responses. Such a bias could have important consequences for decision making by police officers and other authorities interacting with racial minorities. The bias requires no intentional racial animus, occurring even for those who are actively trying to avoid it. This research thus raises difficult questions about intent and responsibility for racially biased errors.

The presumption that a person from one racial group may be more dangerous than another is discriminatory because information about a group is being substituted for information about the individual, a phenomenon known as statistical discrimination (Thurow 1975). Statistical discrimination is distinguished from preference discrimination (Becker 1957), which measures the additional cost one would pay not to interact with members of another group. The Civil Rights Act of 1964 makes both kinds of discrimination illegal, but market competition will eliminate only preference discrimination.

Problems in eliminating statistical discrimination motivate the use of quotas in things like university admissions and lending transactions. In these contexts, the cost of seeking specific information about individuals is both recognized and legally assigned to one party or the other. An applicant might, for example, be required to pay a fee to have transcripts sent or to run a credit check. In either case, assigning the cost of information search to the decision body is problematic because that cost could motivate discriminating behavior (e.g., using a rule of thumb criteria) to save the search expense.

Presuppositional Complexity

Identifying the source of a presupposition in cases of discrimination is important in mitigating a problem. In cases of statistical discrimination, the response might be to require additional information, as in university admissions. In cases of preference discrimination, stiffer penalties could provide relief. Assuming preference discrimination in cases involving statistical discrimination is unlikely to solve the underlying problem.

A troubling alternative explanation is that the upward mobility of ethnic minorities makes it more likely that now they live outside of ethic ghettos. This success makes it more likely that they will interact with blue-collar police of another ethnicity who resent their success and act on their resentment. The perceived ethic bias then is, in fact, a façade over class conflict that adds another layer of complexity to presuppositions that can easily be misdiagnosed. If class conflict is masquerading as ethic bias in the case of police shootings, then hiring a minority police chief may increase rather than lower tensions with the community because it draws attention to a lack of promotion potential for already embittered police.

Church Attendance and Biblical Interpretation

Presuppositions influence our attitude about church attendance and how we read our Bibles. For most Americans in the 1950s, American culture presumed that women worked primarily in the home and families attended church on Sundays, an assumption with deeply held roots. Wells (1993, 26–27) writes:

> Moralists and campaigners in the nineteenth century [1830s] almost invariable addressed their pleas and admonitions to women, to the hands that rocked the cradles. Men, in seemed, were beyond redemption unless their womenfolk

could get to them. Carousing and cavorting were accepted as an inevitable part of being male, but it was felt that if women were in the some way to fall as well, the very fabric of society would be rent.

The *"blue laws"* mandated that most retail stores were not open on Sunday. In my grandfather's home town, a farmer harvesting his corn on Sunday would likely have received a pastoral visit the following week. Today, stores are legally open seven days a week because the culture presumes that women and men both work during the week away from the home and church attendance is no longer assumed.[4]

Biblical interpretation is also informed by our cultural presuppositions. Today, for example, many people read their Bibles but are skeptical about the miraculous events that are recorded. Behind this skepticism is the metaphysical presupposition that the physical world is the only world, and science has not been able to reproduce many of the miracles recorded in the Bible. Unable to accept the miracles of the Bible, in 1820 Thomas Jefferson famously abstracted the miracles from the four Gospels to create his own Bible, which is today on display at the National Museum of American History in Washington DC.[5]

For example, Luke 10 reports that Jesus restored the sight to a blind Bartimaeus (Luke 10:46–52). Was the miracle the restoration of sight or something else, like a restoration of faith? If Jesus restored Bartimaeus' sight, then Jesus' status as the Son of God is validated. If he merely restored his faith, Jesus may be nothing more than a great teacher or prophet, as many have claimed.

Christians who have experienced God's mercy and love first-hand in their lives have no problem believing that Bartimaeus had his sight restored, a counter-cultural presupposition. How do you interpret the miracles recorded in the Bible?

The Role of Authorities in Decisions

*L*et's return for a moment to my decision as a college student to follow my father into the economics profession. When I made this decision, I had no idea what an economist could expect to earn and whether studying economics posed a profitable investment decision. What I knew was that my father had studied economics and was able to earn a living. This implies that my decision was no entirely rational.

Note that I made this decision under duress—I had labored anxiously for months without direction. On the morning that I made this decision, I had a bad hangover. These are not ideal conditions for making major life decisions and bring to mind the circumstances facing the Prodigal Son (Luke 15:11–32). Still, I took it on faith that if I followed my father into the economics profession, I would earn a similar income and be able to support a family. In a formal sense, I did not make a rational decision based on current expected earnings in the economics profession.

Rationality of Decisions Based on Authority

Two important points can be made about my decision to study economics.

The first point is that most decisions are made within

a context of high levels of uncertainty—the future is always uncertain. Uncertainty motivates the gathering of additional information. Because information is costly and time–consuming, the search process is often constrained by the limits of our budget (both money and time). When no limit is imposed, analysis paralysis can arise if we have trouble coping with uncertainty and making decisions.

The second point is that the use of authorities in the decision process provides an obvious short-cut to searching for more information. While some may not languish over decisions but simply adopt the advice of others to avoid the anxiety of decision-making, this was not a motivator for me. I knew that if I studied economics, my father could advise me on what to do and what not to do along the way, reducing my decision risk. In a sense, I became an apprentice to my father. Being an apprentice, therefore, not only cut my search costs in making the initial decision, but also the prospective costs in making future career decisions.

If I chose another field to study, I could have gotten the same benefits by seeking out mentors to guide through difficult decisions along the way. In fact, when I moved in my career to finance, I did exactly that. Although I changed positions repeatedly in my government career, I always sought mentors to guide my decisions.

Christ as Mentor

In a sense, placing our faith in God is analogous to taking Christ as our mentor. When we come to faith, our information set may be minimal, but we know that God is good and is trustworthy. By trusting God and taking Christ as our guide, we can avoid many of the pitfalls that come with inexperience as decision-makers in this life.

But there is one other important point to make. As Christians, we know that the future is in Christ (John 14:1–3). Knowing the end of the story reduces the uncertainty that we face in this life. Thus, we not only benefit from the guidance of our mentor, but he reduces our uncertainty. It is like we already have tomorrow's newspaper and know today which stock will go up.

WHO IS GOD?

Overview

*I*n the previous review of information, learning, and decision-making, what stands out is how unlikely it is that we should encounter God and come to faith on our own. The Good News of the Bible is that God seeks us out and reveals himself to us in spite of numerous obstacles.

In his self-disclosure to Moses, God describes himself in terms of virtues—merciful, gracious, patient, loving, and faithful (Exod 34:6)—and relates to his people primarily through covenants and his written word. God further reveals himself in three persons: Father, Son, and Holy Spirit. We experience him both in his transcendence (God above) and immanence (God with us).

Because of original sin and our limitations as human beings, learning is an important aspect of our decisions and who we are. God is sinless and is not subject to our limitations. Because God stands outside of time and space, his character is immutable relative to us. This implies that he does not learn as we do.

Being created in God's image implies that we should emulate God's ethical character as a model for our own lives.

When we sin, we idolize other persons and things, and try to redefine God's covenantal love to serve our own needs.

Origin of the Bible

*T*he Bible describes the history of God's relationship with humanity, so it is important to understand the Bible's origins.

In the Koran, Christians are described as people of the book. This is not surprising because the New Testament was the first bound book (Stone 2010, 11). Books were cheaper to produce and more portable than the scrolls that recorded the Hebrew Bible. More New Testament manuscripts have survived from ancient times than any other ancient text.[1]

Background

In his Easter letter of AD 367, Athanasius suggested the twenty-seven books of the New Testament that the Council of Carthage confirmed as canonical in AD 397. Athanasius chose these books because their authors either were apostles of Christ or worked closely with one.

In AD 382, Pope Damasus I commissioned Jerome to prepare an authoritative translation of the Bible into Latin (the Hebrew Scriptures plus the New Testament), which is commonly known as the Vulgate (Evans 2005, 162). The Vulgate remained the authoritative Biblical translation for the church until the time of the Reformation, when the reformers began translating the

Bible into common languages.

Reformation

In 1522, reformer Martin Luther translated the New Testament into German and followed with an Old Testament translation a decade later.[2] Luther kept the twenty-seven books of the New Testament, but followed the Masoretic (Hebrew Old Testament) rather than the Septuagint (Greek Old Testament) in selecting books for the Old Testament.[3]

The books left out of the Masoretic text but included in the Septuagint became known as the Apocrypha. These books continue to distinguish the Catholic (Apocrypha included) from Protestant Bible translations (Apocrypha excluded) to this day. The list of books in the Bible given below, which excludes the Apocrypha, is taken from the Westminster Confession:

OLD TESTAMENT

Genesis, Exodus, Leviticus, Numbers, Deuteronomy, Joshua, Judges, Ruth, 1 Samuel, 2 Samuel, 1 Kings, 2 Kings, 1 Chronicles, 2 Chronicles, Ezra, Nehemiah, Esther, Job, Psalms, Proverbs, Ecclesiastes, Song of Solomon, Isaiah, Jeremiah, Lamentations, Ezekiel, Daniel, Hosea, Joel, Amos, Obadiah, Jonah, Micah, Nahum, Habakkuk, Zephaniah, Haggai, Zechariah, Malachi.

NEW TESTAMENT

Matthew, Mark, Luke, John, Acts, Romans, 1 Corinthians, 2 Corinthians, Galatians, Ephesians, Colossians, Philippians, 1 Thessalonians, 2 Thessalonians, 1 Timothy, 2 Timothy, Titus, Philemon, Hebrews, James, 1 Peter, 2 Peter, 1 John, 2 John, 3 John, Jude, Revelation.

Reading the Bible

When we study of the Bible, Jesus' attitude about scripture guides our thinking. Jesus said:

> Do not think that I have come to abolish the Law or the Prophets; I have not come to abolish them but to fulfill them. For truly, I say to you, until heaven and earth pass away, not an iota, not a dot, will pass from the Law until all is accomplished. (Matt 5:17–18)

The Law of Moses refers to the Law (first five books of the Bible) and the Prophets refers to the other books of the Old Testament.

The last book in the Old Testament to be written was likely Malachi, which was written about four hundred years before the birth of Christ. The last book in the New Testament to be written was likely the book of Revelation which was written around AD ninety.

The Bible represents the work of many authors, yet its contents are uniquely consistent, which adds weight to our belief that the Bible was inspired by the Holy Spirit (2 Tim 3:16–17).

Interpreting the Bible

The critical role of the Bible in Christian faith, thought, and life makes it important to interpret it accurately. The Bible poses at least three hermeneutical (interpretational) challenges to a modern reader.

Interpretational Challenges

First, the Bible is only ancient text that most people ever read. The writers of the New Testament wrote roughly two thousand years ago and referenced Old Testament texts written over a period from two thousand to several hundred years prior to that point. Does our inexperience with ancient texts imply that only experts can read the Bible correctly? Historically, the Roman Catholic Church insisted that only the Church could correctly interpret scripture,[1] while Protestants insisted that the plain meaning (perspicuity or clarity) of scripture was obvious enough that common people could interpret the Bible (Sprout 1977, 15).

Second, the ancient source of the Bible implies that these authors lived in cultural contexts vastly different from our own and they wrote in unfamiliar languages—principally Hebrew and Greek.[2] Both the cultures and the languages influence translation, requiring assumptions to be made that significantly impact the translated text. For example, should the translator translate each word (New American Standard Bible) or translate the meaning of a paragraph (The Message Bible)? Should the translator assume that the text has been written for formal settings (King James Bible) or for everyday use (Good News Bible)?

Third, the Bible is a compilation of books written by different authors in a wide range of genres. Genesis, for example, mostly records historical narratives while Exodus combines narrative with law. The witness of the church attributes both books to Moses who, as a major participant in Exodus, might be considered to be writing a memoir. But since the Book of Deuteronomy, another book attributed to Moses, records Moses' death (Deut 34:5), it might be more appropriate to attribute the Pentateuch (the five books of Moses or the Books of the Law) to the Moses administration. Even though Mosaic authorship was not questioned until the nineteenth century, even the meaning of Moses' authorship requires interpretation.

Similar problems arise in determining genre. For example, what genre are we reading when we read:

> Now the serpent was more crafty than any other
> beast of the field that the LORD God had made.
> He said to the woman, Did God actually say, You
> shall not eat of any tree in the garden? (Gen 3:1)

Is this verse simple narrative, a metaphor, or a fable? Depending on your prior convictions, you may interpret this verse differently, which is an important reason to consider genre.

Biblical Keys to Interpretation

Although most Christians discount the importance of hermeneutics (the study of interpretation), hermeneutic concerns defined Christian denominations historically and lie at the heart of numerous controversies today. The mere observation that seminarians require intense training in the languages of the Bible speaks to the subtly of scripture and the need to understand those subtleties. Less frequently noted, however, are hermeneutical keys given in the Bible itself.

For example, after God gives Moses the Ten Commandments (the second time), God reveals his character:

> The LORD passed before him and proclaimed, The LORD, the LORD, a God merciful and gracious, slow to anger, and abounding in steadfast love and faithfulness, keeping steadfast love for thousands, forgiving iniquity and transgression and sin, but who will by no means clear the guilty, visiting the iniquity of the fathers on the children and the children's children, to the third and the fourth generation. (Exod 34:6–7)

God's character is critical in interpreting the commandments wherever a question arises. Note, for example, that God is first described as merciful—not punishing as deserved—then being described as a gracious—rewarding with undeserved blessings. God is a merciful and gracious lawgiver, which is helpful to know in understanding the atonement of Christ (1 Cor 15:3) or if you are charged with implementing God's law in your own community.

Much like God reveals his character to Moses as an interpretative key, Jesus gives us an interpretative key immediately after introducing the Beatitudes, the introduction to his Sermon on Mount.

> Do not think that I have come to abolish the Law or the Prophets; I have not come to abolish them but to fulfill them. For truly, I say to you, until heaven and earth pass away, not an iota, not a dot, will pass from the Law until all is accomplished. Therefore whoever relaxes one of the least of these commandments and teaches others to do the same will be called least in the kingdom of heaven, but whoever does them and teaches them will be called great in the kingdom of heaven. (Matt 5:17–19)

The phrase, the Law and the Prophets, is a euphemism for the Old Testament that implies Jesus expects his followers to reference the Old Testament when they interpret his teaching. This admonishment comes as a warning to those who prefer to pick a favorite saying of Jesus and use it to discount Old Testament teaching, as is commonly done today (e.g., Rogers 2009, 52–65).

A contemporary example of these interpretative keys is the idea of a conference report. Whenever the U.S. Congress passes important legislation, the staff responsible write a conference report that explains how key elements of the legislation came together and why. Lawyers inside and outside the government then refer to the conference report whenever questions arise on how to interpret the law.

In its use as an ancient conference report, Exodus 34:6 is repeatedly mentioned elsewhere in scripture.[3] For example, the Prophet Jonah refused God's command to preach to the Ninevites because he hated them, wanted their city to be destroyed, and knew that God would forgive them if they responded to his preaching (Jonah 4:2). Jesus specifically references this passage in Jonah (Luke 11:29–32; Matt 12:39–41)

The Need for Context

Taking scripture out of context is the single, most important misuse of scripture. Context, according to Schultz (2012, 40–41),

> refers to the flow of thought in a passage, for example, how a specific sentence is related to the sentences that precede and follow it.

He cites four types of biblical context:

1. Literary context—the *"text surrounding an individual verse or passage."*

2. Historical-Cultural Context—biblical authors wrote with a particular readership in mind, who share a common knowledge of key events in Israelite History, religious practices and core theological beliefs.

3. Salvation-Historical Context—the Bible: offers one extensive 'story' (today sometimes called 'macronarrative' [or meta-narrative]), which stretches from the creation to the consummation of human history, as we know it, climaxing in the creation of a new heaven and new earth.

4. Theological-Thematic Context—"*When studying a text, it is helpful to identify its dominant themes...*" (Schultz 2012, 52)

Schultz observes that the tendency among those who misuse scripture is to ignore the context of the passage being cited and to substitute their own context, which may or may not correspond to the original context and meaning in scripture.

Vanhoozer (1998, 25–29) sees the three key contexts for interpreting scripture as the author, other scripture, and the reader. The author's context focuses on the intent, social context, and audience of the writer. The context of other scripture shares the divine inspiration of any particular text; if something in one place is unclear, perhaps it is clearer somewhere else. The reader's context, when balanced against the other two, provides a valid expression of the Holy Spirit's inspiration in our own lives.

In response to recent postmodern critiques of scripture, Vanhoozer observes:

> My thesis is that ethical interpretation is a spiritual exercise and that the spirit of understanding is not a spirit of power, nor of play, but the Holy Spirit.

If interpretation becomes a power play, clearly divine inspiration is not the prime motivator and the reader's context may simply be another attempt to insert our own context for that of the text.

How to Interpret Scripture Properly

Schultz goes on to offer seven suggestions for interpreting scripture properly:

1. Care about understanding.

2. Catch nuance.

3. Clarify context.

4. Check terms.

5. Consider genre.

6. Consult expert [texts].

7. Correlate application [with text]. (Schultz 2012, 139–140).

Schultz's first point is instructive. In seminary, I found studying scripture in the original languages to be an eye-opener, in part, because the texts were too familiar—I thought that I knew what the text was saying, but often missed the nuances, details, and even the main point of a passage. Reading in Greek or Hebrew forced me to slow down and consider each word carefully.

Scripture haa a minimum of words (is laconic), so each word serves a particular purpose.

Interpreting the Bible 2.0

> *Then the LORD God said,*
> *it is not good that the man should be alone;*
> *I will make him a helper (עֵזֶר) fit for him.*
> *(Gen 2:18)*

*E*arlier I noted how important hermeneutics is to understanding scripture, distinguishing Christian groups, and sorting out controversies in the church. Here I focus on interpreting one verse, Genesis 2:18, cited above. In this verse, God talks about creating Eve and refers to her as Adam's helper.

A Patriarchal Read?

Historically, Genesis 2:18 has been used to justify the husband's authority over the wife in the marriage relationship. Other support typically cited is Adam naming Eve, another sign of authority (Gen 2:23), and Eve yielding to Satan's temptation (Gen 3:6), a sign taken as weakness on her part (1 Tim 2:14).

An alternative interpretation notes that Adam and Eve are created together as a pair: "*So God created man in his own image, in the image of God he created him; male and female he created them.*" (Gen 1:27) Later, in marriage, a man is to give up his father's household to live with his wife (Gen 2:24), which was not the typical custom among other people groups in the Ancient Near East. Further, if one reads the temptation narrative closely, Adam is standing next to Eve when Satan tempts her. If he is truly *the man of the house*, then why does he stand there mute while his wife is talking to a snake? Is the snake addressing the boss?

Key to this patriarchal interpretation is the word translated as helper (עֵזֶר; ezer). While helper can sometimes mean a slave, more typically it refers to a higher status person or even God himself: *"Behold, God is my helper (עֹזֵר); the Lord is the upholder of my life."* (Ps 54:4) Webb (2001, 128) writes:

> A survey of the Hebrew world for 'helper' (ezer) should caution against using the word itself to support either position. When including both the noun and verb forms, there are about 128 occurrences in the Old Testament. The majority of uses (72%) are of superior-status individuals helping these of a lesser status. Yet, there are a number of examples where the 'helper' is either of equal status (18%) or of lower status (10%) than the one being helped…Only contextual factors beyond the word should be used to establish [status].

In other words, Webb is arguing that the word *helper* is ambiguous about the relative status of Adam and Eve. Readers of the passage are likewise divided. However, in scripture we find a clear statement by the Apostle Paul: *"There is neither Jew nor Greek, there is neither slave nor free, there is no male and female, for you are all one in Christ Jesus."* (Gal 3:28) While some commentators will debate Paul's commitment to equality, his comments on family relations in Ephesians 6:1–9 completely undermined the patriarchal system of his time, when the father's rights over women, children, and slaves were absolute.

The early church functioned as a de facto family group, which is why terms like brother and sister are used throughout the New Testament and even today to refer to fellow believers. This suggests that equality among the members under the fatherhood of God was a dominant virtue in the church. Hellerman (2001, 221) observes:

> those who had the most to gain from the image of the church as a family were the poor, the hungry, the enslaved, the imprisoned, the orphans, and the widows. For brother-sister terminology in antiquity had nothing to with hierarchy, power, and privilege, but everything to do with equality, solidarity, and generalized reciprocity.

This is an important finding because many writers today allege incorrectly that the patrilineal kinship group model is used rhetorically to promote hierarchy at the expense of socially disadvantaged groups.

Adam and Eve or Adam and Steve?

After many years of Evangelicals saying that God created Adam and Eve, not Adam and Steve, gay commentators jokingly began turning this argument around.[1] If the Great Commandment (love neighbor, love God; Matt 22:36–40) is true and should be our ethical and interpretative guide as Christians as advocated, for example, by Rogers (2009, 65) , then sometimes the perfect helper for Adam is Steve, not Eve. If Adam loves Steve, who is to say it is not so? After all, God had just introduced him to all the living creatures and birds of the air, looking presumably for a helper for Adam (Gen 2:18–20).

Why might we find this interpretation unconvincing? Two reasons suggest that this is a speculative reading.

First, the author of the passage, Moses, uses these verses (Gen 2:18–20) as a foil to introduce Eve and Adam as happy with God's new creation:

> Then the man said, This at last is bone of my bones
> and flesh of my flesh; she shall be called Woman,
> because she was taken out of Man. (Gen 2:23)

The immediate context of the passage rules out any substitutes for Eve.

Second, if any confusion existed on how to interpret Genesis 2:18, then Leviticus 18:22 explicitly and unequivocally forbids homosexual relationships.[2] Because Moses wrote both Genesis and Leviticus, one would need to argue that Moses disagreed with himself or changed his mind, which seems unlikely.

Looking to the New Testament for further guidance, the Apostle Paul refers to homosexuality and lesbianism both as a curse for rejecting God and his self-identification in creation (Rom 1:19–28). In this context love means accepting people as they are, but caring enough to help them to move beyond their fallen state, as Jesus does with the woman caught in adultery (John 8).

Why Bother Talking About Hermeneutics?

The point of these examples is to encourage Christians to take scriptural interpretation seriously. Weak or unusual interpretations typically either take scripture out of context or focus exclusively on a reader context. Considering also the author's intent and the wider scriptural context generally provide a more balanced reading than talking exclusively about a reader interpretation.

God's Attributes in Creation

*T*he Bible starts telling us that: *"In the beginning, God cre-ated the heavens and the earth."* (Gen 1:1) What do these simple words tell us about God?

Eternal

The phrase *in the beginning* tells us that God is eternal. If creation has a beginning, then it must also have an end. This implies that creation is not eternal, but the God who created it must be. If our eternal God created time, both the beginning and the end, then everything God created belongs to God. Just as the potter is master over the pottery he makes, God is sovereign over creation (Jer 18:4–6). God did not win creation in an arm-wrestling match, find it on the street, or buy it online; he created it—God is a worker (Whelchel 2012, 7).

Transcendent

Having created the universe, God stands outside of time and space, which is what it means to be eternal and transcendent (Gen 1:1). The immediate consequence of God's transcendence is that as mortal beings we cannot approach God without his assistance.

The Tower of Babel narrative is the Bible's preeminent transcendence story (Gen 11:1–9). In the story, men tried to build a tower to heaven intending to force God to come down and bless their city. The text reads:

> Come, let us build ourselves a city and a tower with its top in the heavens, and let us make a name for ourselves, lest we be dispersed over the face of the whole earth. (Gen 11:4)

The phrase *make a name for ourselves* suggests an attempt to gain sovereignty over God, while the reference to the word *dispersed* suggests disobedience to God's command to *"Be fruitful and multiply and fill the earth and subdue it."* (Gen 1:28)

We can imagine God looking down from heaven and just laughing at these foolish men because he immediately does away with this building project by confusing them with different languages. Yet, the Tower of Babel in a physical sense provides a metaphor for philosophical towers that we have more recently attempted to build, such as the Enlightenment Project.[1]

Sovereignty

God's sovereignty is reinforced in the second half of Genesis 1:1 when it says: God created the heavens and the earth. Here heaven and earth form a poetic construction called a merism. A merism is a literary device that can be compared to defining a line segment by referring to its end points. The expression—heaven and earth—therefore means that God created everything.[2]

Because he created everything, he is sovereign over creation; and sovereignty implies ownership.[3]

Holy

So, from the first sentence in the Bible we know that God is eternal and he is sovereign, but we also know that he is holy. Why? Are heaven and earth equal? No. Heaven is God's residence. From the story of Moses' encounter with God in the burning bush (Exod 3:5), we learn that any place where God is becomes holy in the sense of being set apart or sacred. Because God resides in heaven, it must be holy. Earth is not. Still, God created both and is sovereign over both (Rev 4:11).

Genesis paints two other important pictures of God.

Holy Spirit

The first picture arises in Genesis 1:2; here the breath, or spirit of God, is pictured like a bird hovering over the waters.[4] Hovering requires time and effort suggesting ongoing participation in and care for creation. The Bible speaks exhaustively about God providing for us—God's provision. Breath translates as Holy Spirit in both Greek (πνεῦμα; pneuma) and Hebrew (רוּחַ; ruha).

Immanence

The second picture appears in Genesis 2, which retells the story of creation in more personal terms. As a potter works with clay

(Isa 64:8), God forms Adam and puts him in a garden where he walks and talks with him directly, an Old Testament allusion to Christ. Then, he talks to Adam and directs him to give the animals names. And when Adam gets lonely, God creates Eve from Adam's rib or side—a place close to his heart.

An allusion to the birth of Christ is given in Genesis 3 in the curse of Satan:

> The LORD God said to the serpent, because you have done this, cursed are you above all livestock and above all beasts of the field; on your belly you shall go, and dust you shall eat all the days of your life. I will put enmity between you and the woman, and between your offspring and her offspring; he shall bruise your head, and you shall bruise his heel. (Gen 3:14–15)

The enmity between the offspring of the woman and Satan is believed to be the first biblical reference both to Christ and to spiritual warfare.

Trinity

Genesis 1 and 2, accordingly, paint three pictures of God: God as a mighty creator; God who meticulously attends to his creation; and God who walks with us like a friend. While the Trinity is not fully articulated in scripture until the New Testament, God's self-disclosure as the Trinity appears from the beginning (Chan 1998, 41).

The Lord's Prayer casts a new perspective on Genesis 1:1 when Jesus says: *"Your kingdom come, your will be done, on earth as it is in heaven."* (Matt 6:10) Because we are created in God's image, we want our home to modeled after God's, a reference to image theology.

Image Theology

*W*hat does it mean to be created in the image of God as male and female?

The Image

Let's start with the reference in the Book of Genesis:

> Then God said, let us make man in our image, after our likeness. And let them have dominion over the fish of the sea and over the birds of the heavens and over the livestock and over all the earth and over every creeping thing that creeps on the earth. So God created man in his own image, in the image of God he created him; male and female he created them. And God blessed them. And God said to them, be fruitful and multiply and fill the earth and subdue it, and have dominion over the fish of the sea and over the birds of the heavens and over every living thing that moves on the earth. (Gen 1:26–28)

The context here is important. We are in the first chapter of the first book in the Bible, so every implied by these three verses about what it means to be created in the image of God has to appear in the prior verses. How does the text describe God?[1]

Consider these four attributes:

1. Verse one tells us that God is a creator who, being eternal, sovereignly stands outside time and space, as discussed previously.

2. Verse two shows us that God can through his spirit enter into his creation.

3. Having created heaven and earth, verse three describes God speaking to shape the form of creation beginning with light Note the exact correspondence between what God says ("Let there be light") and what he does ("and there was light")—God is truthful, authentic.

4. Verse four tells us that God judged it to be good, and he separated it from darkness—God discriminates good (light) from the not-so-good (darkness).

Clearly, God cares about ethics.

The Ethical Image

God later describes his ethical character in detail to Moses after giving the Ten Commandments a second time, as cited earlier in Exodus 34:6. God's self-disclosure was important for understanding how to interpret the Ten Commandments, should questions arise, but it also underscores the creation account providing insight into whose image we are created to reflect.

Going back to Genesis 1:26–28, two aspects of God's image are highlighted in our own creation description. We are created by a sovereign God who creates us to participate in his creation in two specific ways: we are to *"have dominion"* over the created order and we are to *"be fruitful and multiply."* How are we to accomplish these things? Following God's ethical image, we are to be discerning of the good, merciful, gracious, patient, loving, and truthful.

The Charge

Although God created animals prior to Adam and Eve and they were also commanded to *"be fruitful and multiply"* (Gen 1:22), the animals could not reflect God's ethical image and God did not give them dominion.

At this point in Genesis, God also intended us also to share in his eternal nature. However, before God conferred immortality on us, he posed an ethical test. Would Adam and Eve reflect God's ethical nature?

The Test

The test came in the form of a command:

> And the LORD God commanded the man, saying, you may surely eat of every tree of the garden, but of the tree of the knowledge of good and evil you shall not eat, for in the day that you eat of it you shall surely die. (Gen 2:16–17)

Satan tempted Adam and Eve to eat of the tree of the knowledge of good and evil, and they ate. Because Satan had done this, God cursed him:

> I will put enmity between you and the woman, and between your offspring and her offspring; he shall bruise your head, and you shall bruise his heel. (Gen 3:15)

The *"he"* in this verse is singular and points to a future redeemer

(Job 19:25), who Christians identify as Jesus Christ (John 1:1–3). After this point in the narrative, God cast Adam and Eve out of the Garden of Eden, where they were subject to the curse of death. We thus see that the original sin of Adam and Eve separated us from the Garden of Eden, eternal life, and fully reflecting the image of God.

Image Theology

Jesus underscores this image theology in several important ways.

First, he is revealed as the ethical image of God with God during creation:

> He [Jesus] was in the beginning with God. All things were made through him, and without him was not anything made that was made. In him was life, and the life was the light of men. The light shines in the darkness, and the darkness has not overcome it. (John. 1:2–5)

Second, Jesus uses image theology in teaching prayer to his disciples: *"Your kingdom come, your will be done, on earth as it is in heaven."* (Matt 6:10) In this phrase, the word *kingdom* is a commonly used circumlocution to avoid referencing God directly, which in the Jewish faith was considered too holy to be used in common language. In the Old Testament, for example, we often see the term, Lord (*adonai* in Hebrew), used instead of God's covenant name, YHWH, often pronounced Yahweh.

Third, just like Jesus asserts God's sovereignty over heaven and hell in his death on the cross, the disciples are commissioned to assert God's sovereignty over the earth after the ascension (Matt 28:18). Right before he ascended, Jesus said:

> But you will receive power when the Holy Spirit has come upon you, and you will be my witnesses in Jerusalem and in all Judea and Samaria, and to the end of the earth. (Acts 1:8)

Parallel Ministry

This parallel ministry is also discussed in John's Gospel: *"As the Father has sent me, even so I am sending you."* (John 20:21) In other words, the Great Commission in Matthew 28:19, *"Go therefore and make disciples of all nations…"*, is not an incidental footnote in Jesus' ministry or a latter addition to the text as some allege, it is a direct consequence of the image theology in Genesis 1. Likewise in the Apostle Paul's writing we see a dichotomy between a putting off of the old self and a putting on of the new self in Christ (Eph 4:22–24), as we are transformed by the image of the living God.

God's Immutability

God is not man, that he should lie, or a son of man,
that he should change his mind.
Has he said, and will he not do it?
Or has he spoken, and will he not fulfill it?
(Num 23:19)

God's unchanging character, his immutability, is not revealed in scripture in the creation accounts directly, but it is implied by his status as creator. In order to create, one needs to stand outside of that being created. When God created the universe, he stood outside of the time and space of the universe. While the universe had a beginning and will have an end, God is eternal. While God's internal nature is veiled to us, his character is immutable relative to his creation.

God's Meekness

God's immutability is also implied by his attribute of being omniscient. Because God is omniscient, he does not need to learn as we do.

The attribute of meekness appears in the Third Beatitude only in Matthew and in the Greek, the language of the New Testament, meek means: *"Not [being] overly impressed with a sense of self-importance, gentle, humble, considerate"* (BDAG 6132). Meek is like poor in spirit, which we find in the First

Beatitude, and at least three other times in Matthew (e.g., Matt 11:29; 21:5; 26:62–63). These three events—the invitation of Jesus to be disciple, his humble entrance into Jerusalem, and his silence during his trial—demonstrate the humility of Christ. The humility of Christ is also observed in the writings of the Apostles—Peter, James, and Paul.

From this evidence, it is obvious that humility is important to Jesus in the New Testament. But no one normally wants to be humble—we have to learn to be humble. Is it possible that God also learned to be humble?

No. God did not learn to be humble, and we are told at least twice in the Old Testament that God does not change (Num 23:19; Mal 3:6).

More specifically, God appears meek and gentle. For example, in Genesis before *"God sent him [Adam and Eve} out from the garden of Eden"* (Gen 3:23), *"God made for Adam and for his wife garments of skins and clothed them"* (Gen 3:21), like a mother prepares her kids for the first day of school. God had every right as creator to kill them both and create new people, but he did not do that. He did not do that because he had compassion on them and made provision for them, in spite their sins and against his own rights and power. In this context, God seems meek both in the Old and New Testament because he does not change and has no need to learn.[1] As we read: *"Jesus Christ is the same yesterday and today and forever."* (Heb 13:8)

From God's constancy and consistency, we draw strength: *"those who trust in the LORD are like Mount Zion, which cannot be moved, but abides forever."* (Ps 125:1)

God Does Not Change Like Us

Tozer (2014, 63) writes:

> To say that God is immutable is to say that He never differs from Himself...[He never goes] from better to worse or from worse to better... [or] change within himself.

Again, standing outside of time and space God sees all of human history before him. We change and grow, but God's character remains immutable. By contrast, confronted with an unmovable, immutable Holy God, we must change. This is why every divine appointment transforms us.

We Care a Lot About God's Immutability

It is fashionable to argue that God somehow learns like we do. Frequently, it is said that the God of the Old Testament is full of wrath and vengeful, while the God of the New Testament is loving, but this interpretation inconveniently suggests that God could continue to change. What if God decided that he made a big mistake in creation, forgot about his promise to Noah, and sends another flood? (Gen 9–17) Or what it God decided that the atonement of Christ was a mistake? (1 Cor 15:2–3) Clearly, God promises are tied to his immutable character (Exod 34:6). Otherwise, our assurance of salvation would be about as permanent as one's name written in sand on a beach.

Context for God's Love

> *Be holy, for I the LORD your God am holy.*
>
> *(Lev 19:2)*

*T*he ethical image of God is a hot-button issue today because of the proclivity of many pastors and Christians to view God exclusively through the lens of love, as we read repeatedly through the writings of the Apostle John: *"Anyone who does not love does not know God, because God is love."* (1 John 4:8). Matthew's double love command is likewise frequently cited:

> Teacher, which is the great commandment in the Law? And he said to him, You shall love the Lord your God with all your heart and with all your soul and with all your mind. This is the great and first commandment. And a second is like it: You shall love your neighbor as yourself. On these two commandments depend all the Law and the Prophets. (Matt 22:36–40)

The Greek word for love (ἀγαπάω) is the same in John and Matthew, and means *"to have a warm regard for and interest in another, cherish, have affection for, love"* (BDAG 38.1). Agape love is clearly distinguished from romantic (*eros*) and brotherly (*philos*) love, because the Greek language has separate words for each.

Love's Confusion

Agape love is less helpful in understanding God's character

because of the wild definitions of love floating around in postmodern culture and the wide scope in Greek usage. Confusion over the meaning of love was already present in the first century, which we know because the Apostle Paul devoted an entire chapter to its definition in his letter to the church at Corinth (1 Cor 13), a city infamous for prostitution.

More useful is focus on the word depend (κρέμαμαι) in Matthew 22:40, which means: *"to cause to hang [like a hinge]."* (BDAG 4395.1), because the Law and the Prophets hang on love, but they also inform love's meaning. The Law and the Prophets inform Matthew's use of the word love.

Covenantal Love

In the Old Testament, God interacts with his people primarily through the giving of covenants. Hafemann (2007, 21) writes:

> God's relationship with the world and his people is not a theoretical abstraction, not is fundamentally a subjective experience. Rather, with salvation history as its framework, this relationship is expressed in and defined by the interrelated covenant that exist through the history of redemption.

Among the many allusions to covenant making in the Bible, none is more detailed than covenant with Moses. After a second giving of the Ten Commandments, we find God revealing his character to Moses in Exodus 34:6, as cited previously. The word translated *"steadfast love"* here (חֶסֶד; *hesed*) means: *"obligation to the community in relation to relatives, friends, guests, master and servants; unity, solidarity, loyalty"* (HOLL). The context makes it clear that the type of love in view here is not a generic agape love, but a more specific covenantal love focused on keeping one's promises.[1] We honor God and our neighbor by treating them with respect and keeping our word, especially when it hurts. This is a heart-felt relationship, but it is more than just a warm, fuzzy feeling.

Bonhoeffer (1976, 50) offers an important insight here:

> No one knows God unless God reveals Himself to him. And so none knows what love is except in the self-revelation of God. Love, then, is the revelation of God.

The fact that mercy, not love, is the first characteristic of God reinforces the idea that love requires an interpretation beyond the agape love that so many cherish. When we say that Jesus died for our sins, we experience his love by means of (or through the instrument of) his mercy. The point that mercy is more primal in the biblical context than love is also reinforced in Jesus' Beatitudes: mercy is listed; love is not (Matt 5:3–11). When we experience God's love through his mercy, covenant-keeping love, not agape love, is in focus.

The Hermeneutics of the New Covenant in Christ

This interpretation of love in Matthew makes particular sense because Matthew views the new covenant in Christ in terms of five commandments. The first commandment is to honor the law and the prophets, that is, the entirety of the Old Testament (Matt 5:18–20). The second has to do with stepping out in faith (Matt 14:28–29). The third instructs the disciples not to obsess about spiritual experiences (Matt 17:9). The fourth instructs then disciples not to pick nits with the law (Matt 19:16–21). The five commandment is the double-love commandment already cited (Matt 22:36–40).

If this set of commandments seems obscure, what we see is Matthew struggling to interpret the new covenant in Christ in an Old Testament framework of specific rules.[2] By contrast, the Apostle John sees the new covenant in terms of the person of Jesus, which is hermetically harder and leads to competing visions of the person of Christ. Whose Jesus are you going to accept?

John Ortberg's Jesus offers an interesting pep-talk to the disciples:

> Here's our strategy. We have no money, no clout,
> no status, no buildings, no soldiers...We will

tell them [Jewish and Romans leaders, Zealots, collaborators, Essenes] all that they are on the wrong track...When they hate us—and a lot of them will...we won't fight back, we won't run away, and we won't give in. We will just keep loving them...That's my strategy. (Ortberg 2008, 107)

Who would have thought that a group using this strategy would even survive the first century, let alone grow to be a world religion? Ortberg's Jesus is one interpretation among many.

Matthew's double love commandment gives us a better idea of how to interpret the person of Christ when it hangs on our understanding of the Old Testament (Matt 5:18–20). It also pre-empts attempts to read the entire Bible in terms of a licentious interpretation of the double-love command (e.g., Rogers 2009, 52–65).

Imitators of God

The Apostle Paul gives a more complete understanding of love in passages where he makes image theology explicit, as when he writes: *"Therefore be imitators of God, as beloved children."* (Eph. 5:1) Paul draws this theme out in more detail in Galatians 5:16–24, where he contrasts the works of the flesh with the fruits of the spirit, echoing God's self-revelation in Exodus 34:6, as previously cited.

A God Who Listens

I sometimes joke that when we talk to God, secular people call that prayer, but when God talks to us, they call it psychosis. While Christians are accustomed to God answering prayer, one of the most astonishing attributes of God is that he listens. For example, in the Book of Judges, we read:

> And the people of Israel did what was evil in the sight of the LORD. They forgot the LORD their God and served the Baals and the Asheroth. Therefore the anger of the LORD was kindled against Israel, and he sold them into the hand of Cushan-rishathaim king of Mesopotamia. And the people of Israel served Cushan-rishathaim eight years. But when the people of Israel cried out to the LORD, the LORD raised up a deliverer for the people of Israel, who saved them, Othniel the son of Kenaz, Caleb's younger brother. The Spirit of the LORD was upon him, and he judged Israel. He went out to war, and the LORD gave Cushan-rishathaim king of Mesopotamia into his hand. (Jdg 3:7–10)

Brueggemann (2016, 59) records the Deuteronomic cycle: doing evil, angering YHWH enough to produce historical subjugation, crying to the Lord in need, and raising up a deliverer (Deut 30). Crying out to the Lord may seem like a strange prayer, but the point is that God listens to people in their suffering, even when it is well-deserved. As the Apostle Paul writes: *"God shows his love for us in that while we were still sinners, Christ died for us."* (Rom

5:8)

Why does this hearing attribute of God astonish us? Well, if you do not believe that God exists or that he exists but is aloof (only transcendent), then God's attentiveness comes as a complete surprise—why would an almighty God pay attention to an insignificant, little me? The short answer is because he loves you—enough to die for you—like a parent loves their child because you are created in his image.

God's willingness to listen also denotes accountability, as we read:

> You shall not wrong a sojourner [immigrant] or oppress him, for you were sojourners in the land of Egypt. You shall not mistreat any widow or fatherless child. If you do mistreat them, and they cry out to me, I will surely hear their cry, and my wrath will burn, and I will kill you with the sword, and your wives shall become widows and your children fatherless. If you lend money to any of my people with you who is poor, you shall not be like a moneylender to him, and you shall not exact interest from him. If ever you take your neighbor's cloak in pledge, you shall return it to him before the sun goes down, for that is his only covering, and it is his cloak for his body; in what else shall he sleep? And if he cries to me, I will hear, for I am compassionate. (Exod 22:21–27)

Mistreating the immigrant, the widow, the orphan, or the poor can evoke the wrath of a listening and compassionate God. Note the penalty for mistreating widows and orphans—you will die by sword, and your wives and children will suffer without you. Thus, we see that ignoring God does not imply that you can do anything that you want.

The pattern in the Book of Judges is especially interesting because we read: *"Everyone did what was right in his own eyes."* (Jdg 17:6) This description might equally apply to our own times.

A modern example of this accountability might be found in the life of Friedrich Nietzsche. Nietzche, the son of a pastor, philosophized that God is dead, which implied that the Christian foundations of Western morality no longer had any relevance (Hendricks 2018).[1] His work served as the philosophical foundation of the Third Reiche in Germany and communism throughout the world. Both atheist regimes brought about enormous suffering, particularly through the Second World War, but also through concentration camps and widespread starvation.

While some see atheism still on the march, Alister McGrath (2004, 1, 262) dates the heyday of atheism from the fall of the Bastille (1789) to the fall of the Berlin Wall (1989). Atheism is still important in motivating tribalism,[2] but the communist states that exemplified the most important of secular institutions have now mostly folded because they were unable to compete politically or economically with democratic, capitalist countries.

Bonhoeffer (1976, 60) observes:

> Jesus gives His support to those who suffer for the sake of a just cause, even if this cause is not precisely the confession of His name; he takes them under his protection. He accepts responsibility for them, and He lays claim to them.

Could the defeat of Nazi Germany (1945) and the collapse of communism with the fall of the Berlin Wall (1989) be viewed as the wrath of God being poured out because of the suffering that they had caused? Was Nietzche's own insanity (1889) also a random event?[3]

Personally, I think that we serve a God who listens.

Image Theology and Idolatry

*B*eing created in the image of God (Gen 1:27) may sound quaint to postmodern ears, but it becomes terribly important in understanding the implications of idolatry, the worship of images other than God. Think of idolatry as a hierarchy of priorities. The First Commandment makes this point: *"You shall have no other gods before me."* (Exod 20:3)

The Second Commandment reinforces the point of the first one:

> You shall not make for yourself a carved image, or any likeness of anything that is in heaven above, or that is in the earth beneath, or that is in the water under the earth. You shall not bow down to them or serve them, for I the LORD your God am a jealous God, visiting the iniquity of the fathers on the children to the third and the fourth generation of those who hate me, but showing steadfast love to thousands of those who love me and keep my commandments. (Exod 20:4–6)

The focus on carved images suggests pagan temple worship, as the Psalmist makes light of:

> Our God is in the heavens; he does all that he pleases. heir idols are silver and gold, the work of human hands. They have mouths, but do not speak; eyes, but do not see. They have ears, but do not hear; noses, but do not smell. They have hands, but do not feel; feet, but do not walk; and they do not make a sound in their throat. Those

who make them become like them; so do all who trust in them. (Ps 115:3–8)

Idolatry and Priorities

The key verse here is the last one: *"Those who make them become like them."* Image theology implies that we grow to become like the god that we worship, even if we worship idols. Our number-one priority, which is a question of identity and attitude, is effectively our god (Hoekema 1994, 84). Giglio (2003, 13) writes:

> So how do you know where and what you worship? It's easy. You simply follow the trail of your time, your affection, your energy, your money, and your loyalty. At the end of that trail you'll find a throne; and whatever, or whoever, is on that throne is what's of highest value to you. On that throne is what you worship.

Idol worship threatens all that we are because over time we become like the god that we worship.

Idolatry Hampers Spiritual Formation

Focusing only on time, how much time do you spend each week in activities contributing to your spiritual formation as compared with other activities? Many men spend much of their free time in shoot-them-up games, often developed by the armed forces for training soldiers. Is it any wonder that, in spite of the fact that automatic weapons have been available since the 1920s, it is only in the last decade that we have seen a rise in mass shootings in public places in the United States unrelated to any political or economic agenda? Intensive activities form us and become part of our identity—spiritual formation is not the only formation that takes place.

Poor formation leads us to worship idols that let us down. When our idols crash, we experience an existential crisis because we must completely reorganize our priorities, which is never easy (Hos 8:4).

The Problem of Suicide

Consider what happens if your number-one priority is work and you lose your job? In spite of record low unemployment, anxiety, depression, drug addiction, and suicide are at record levels in the United States, and have contributed to a decline in life expectancy (Bernstein 2018).

Amidst the high level of suicide (Tavernise 2016), two age groups stand out: young people under the age of thirty and older white men, a group not historically prone to suicide. Among young people, the typically reason for attempting suicide is a broken relationship (idolizing a person); among older men, the typical reason is a lost job (workaholism). Both problems suggest a tie to idolatry.

Death by suicide is just the tip of the iceberg according to

Mason (2014, 28):

> Based on large national surveys, for every fourteen suicides per hundred thousand people each year, approximately five hundred people attempt suicide and three thousand think about it.

If psychiatric problems, such as addictions, anxiety, and depression, have a spiritual root, then talk therapy and medication can only ease the pain; they cannot solve the problem. A solution requires dealing with the root cause.[1]

God's Love

Because we are created in the image of God and are commanded to love him and only him, God's jealousy is part of his care for us. The Jewish daily prayer, known in Hebrew as the Shema (the name), goes like this:

> Hear, O Israel: The LORD our God, the LORD is one. You shall love the LORD your God with all your heart and with all your soul and with all your might. (Deut 6:4–5)

Loving God above all else serves to vaccinate us from some serious problems.

The Person of Jesus

*T*he role of Jesus Christ that starts with creation: *"In the beginning God created the heavens and the earth."* (Gen 1:1) God had to exist before the universe that he created and stood apart from it, not part of creation. God stands outside of time and space; we do not.

No Path Up the Mountain

The creation account accordingly implies that as mortal beings, we cannot approach an immortal God without his assistance. Worse, our sin also separates us from a Holy God. No path reaches up the mountain to God; God must come down. As Christians, we believe that God came down in the person of Jesus of Nazareth, whose coming was prophesied by the Prophet Job:

> For I know that my Redeemer lives, and at the last he will stand upon the earth. And after my skin has been thus destroyed, yet in my flesh I shall see God, whom I shall see for myself, and my eyes shall behold, and not another. (Job 19:25–27)

The Book of Job is thought by some to have been written by Moses before any other book in the Bible and before he returned to Egypt, which makes the anticipation of a redeemer all the more stunning. Moses himself lived about 1,500 years before Christ.

God's Character is Critical

Who then is this transcendent God that loves us enough to

initiate connection with us in spite of our sin? After giving Moses the Ten Commandments for a second time on Mount Sinai, God reveals himself to Moses in Exodus 34:6, as cited earlier. Notice that God describes himself first as merciful. As Christians, we believe that God love is shown to us through the death and resurrection of Jesus Christ. Because God himself has provided the ultimate sacrifice of his son on the cross, Christians do not need to offer animal sacrifices—in Christ, our debt to God for sin has already been paid (1 Cor 15:3–5). This is real mercy, real love.

Our Great High Priest

Jesus, as the perfect son of God, is the bridge (Gen 28:12) that God has given us to connect with himself, as we read:

> For we do not have a high priest who is unable to sympathize with our weaknesses, but one who in every respect has been tempted as we are, yet without sin. (Heb 4:15)

As Peter said on the Day of Pentecost:

> And Peter said to them, Repent and be baptized every one of you in the name of Jesus Christ for the forgiveness of your sins, and you will receive the gift of the Holy Spirit. (Acts 2:38)

Through the power of the Holy Spirit, we are able to pray to God with the assurance that we will be heard; we are able to read the

Bible with the confidence that God will speak to us; and we are able to live our daily lives knowing that God walks with us each step of the way.

ARGUMENTS ABOUT GOD'S EXISTENCE

Overview

*T*he Bible does not argue the existence of God because virtually everyone in the ancient world believed in gods of some sort. Intellectual arguments for God's existence in the postmodern era seldom provide sufficient evidence to compel belief because heart and mind are not equally engaged. Greek dualism, which stipulates that heart and mind are separate entities, pervades modern and postmodern thinking and weakens apologetics based solely on the heart or the mind.

While traditional culture focuses on loyalty and moderns concentrate on seeking objective truth, postmoderns prefer to ask who has the best story. The proclivity of the Gospel's biggest critics to become believers—when they take the time to understand it—underscores the resilience of the Gospel message. The Gospel is undoubtedly the best story around.

When heart and mind are seen as inseparable, apologetics actually becomes easier. Things like hospitality and raising godly children become important in sharing the Good News.

Hebrew Anthropology and Apologetics

> *Delight yourself in the LORD,*
> *and he will give you the desires of your heart.*
> *(Ps 37:4)*

*P*art of the church's postmodern confusion stems from the Greek dualism that pervades western thought. While the New Testament taught that mind and body are parts of a unified whole whose center is the heart (Hebrew anthropology), Greeks thought of mind and body as separate (Greek anthropology). Confusion arises because postmodern people read the word *heart* in their Bible as a body-part rather than as the center of our being. This distinction in anthropology especially affects our attitudes about thinking and emotion.

Heart and Mind Inseparable

While this subject is timely, it is not new. Theologian Jonathan Edwards (2009, 13), writing in 1746 about the effects of the Great Awakening, noted that both head and heart were necessarily involved in effective discipling. He coined the phrase *holy affections* to distinguish the marks of the work of the Spirit from other works and associated these holy affections directly with scripture.

More recently, Elliott (2009, 46–47) distinguishes two theories of emotions: the cognitive theory and the non-cognitive

170   *Simple Faith*

theory. The cognitive theory of emotions argues that *"reason and emotion are interdependent"* while the non-cognitive theories promote the separation of reason and emotion. In other words, the cognitive theory states that we get emotional about the things that we strongly believe.

Elliott notes that the God of the Bible only gets angry on rare occasions when people have disobeyed the covenant or expressed a hardness of the heart, as in the case of Pharaoh (Exod 4:21). Our emotions are neither random nor unexplained because they are not mere physiology. Elliott (2009, 53–54) writes: *"If the cognitive theory is correct, emotions become an integral part of our reason and our ethics,"* informing and reinforcing moral behavior.

Hebrew Anthropology

Smith (2016, 5) asks: *"Do you ever experience a gap between what you know and what you do?"* If he had only the mind in view, decisions would be easy. Thoughts would translate immediately into actions, something that seldom happens. More typically our thinking and feelings are not in sync as when the Apostle Paul writes: *"For I do not do the good I want, but the evil I do not want is what I keep on doing."* (Rom 7:19)

This line of thought leads Smith (2016, 7) to observe: *"What if you are defined not by what you know [the mind] but by what you desire [the heart]?"* If our desires are reflected more in our actions than in our thoughts, then this Hebrew anthropology leads us immediately into an inconvenient reflection on ethics because our hearts are not as lily-white clean as our thoughts. It also forces us to reflect on how we know what we know (the epistemology question) because our hearts are not easily persuaded to follow our thoughts. Suddenly, the New Testament language sounds less opaque and more informed by an alternative world view, one decidedly not Greek.

Future Always Present

Smith offers an interesting ethical insight—an instrument (or person) is good when it is used with its purpose in view. He asks how one would evaluate a flute used to roast marshmallows over a fire—we would never say that a flute used this way was a bad flute. Why? Because the measure of a flute is how well it plays music, not how well it roasts marshmallows, as he observes:

> Virtue is bound up with a sense of excellence: a virtue is a disposition that inclines us to achieve the good for which we are made. Smith (2016, 88–89)

Because of original sin, we are not inclined to love virtues and to practice them (Rom 7:14–20), as being created in the image of God suggests. Consequently, in worship we are on a mission to develop virtue through ritual and sacrament that reinforce God's intent for our lives in creation.

This sense of worship explains why the Book of Revelation draws many illusions from the creation accounts in Genesis, and paints many pictures of worship in heaven (e.g., Rev 22:1–5). Our collective objective as Christians is to live into our vision of heaven (our eschatology), where we reflect and commune with the God that we worship. Our eschatology is always in view and it informs how we should live and worship (Phil 3:12–16).

But how are we to live into our collective future if we love the wrong things today?

Sacred Liturgies

Smith (2016, 46) spends a lot of time discussing liturgies. He writes: *"Liturgy, as I'm using the word, is a shorthand term for those rituals that are loaded with an ultimate story about who we are and what we're for."* The Apostle's Creed is, for example, both a ritual and a story that explains who Jesus is, who we are, and what we are for. Repeating the creed until you can recite it in your sleep implies that it has become a ritual and a part of your identity.

Holy music goes a step further to bury it in your heart. Having worked with Alzheimer's patients, I can tell you that songs like the Doxology are the last thing you forget before getting lost in the mist—I have seen patients unable to speak brought back to themselves when you sing such songs with them.

The Problem of Secular Liturgies

The problem is that our society—even the shopping mall—has its own liturgies (Smith 2016, 47–53). When you are upset, do you go to chapel and pray (think of the film *Home Alone*),[1] or do you call a friend and go shopping? Why shop? The liturgy of the mall suggests that individuals find empowerment in purchasing things that they probably don't want or need.

Inherent in purchasing things to make us feel good about ourselves is the reality that we are broken and are trying to fill the void within with stuff. While the stuff empowers us to feel good initially, it also sets us up for a comparison with others who have more stuff. So the feel-good benefit quickly wears off because, on reflection, it reveals how shallow we have become (Smith 2016, 47–53).

Hospitality More Than Food

If the heart is the center of our identity, not just our emotions, then we need to think about apologetics differently. An apologetic focused on heart needs to appeal both to the mind and the emotions. Let me offer three examples.

The first example concerns the first letter of Peter, where the most famously quoted verse is: *"Always being prepared to make a defense to anyone who asks you for a reason for the hope that is in you."* (1 Pet 3:15) The thing is that the rest of the book focuses on lifestyle evangelism, as it says:

> Keep your conduct among the Gentiles honorable, so that when they speak against you as evildoers, they may see your good deeds and glorify God on the day of visitation. (1 Pet 2:12)

Works like hospitality speak without words directly to the heart.

The second example arose in the fourth century when Saint Patrick became famous as the first successful evangelist to Ireland. His success was not anticipated because Patrick, as a sixteen-year old, was kidnapped by Irish pirates and sold as a slave in Ireland. For the next six years, he worked as a slave caring for his master's cattle in the Irish wilderness. Later, he escaped and traveled to France to study to become a priest. Much later, he returned to Ireland as a bishop and evangelized the Irish out of love for them. His evangelism focused on offering hospitality. In the end, Patrick and his companions planted more than seven hundred churches in Ireland (Hunter 2000, 13–23).

The third example is more recent. In the city of Rio de Janeiro, there are many young people caught up in the gangs of the drug culture. In Brazil, they call young people with mixed blood (blacks and Indians) as the *"killable people,"* because no one gets upset when they are murdered. Many of them die violent deaths, but those who survive and are incarcerated by the police don't have it much better. In the jails, the police do not feed them or offer medical care. For the most part, the gangs control daily life in the prisons. In this hellish world, there are few visitors, but those that come are mostly Pentecostals who provide food, medicine, and worship services. As a consequence, the gangs respect the Pentecostals, providing security for their services and allowing young people who really come to Christ to leave the gangs—the only escape other than in a body bag (Johnson 2017).

As we have seen, hospitality can be more than just food. In these stories, it can be a faith journey that travels the path to the Hebrew heart.

The Surprising Role of Storytelling

*P*ostmodernism is often compared to a collage, a hanging ornament with unique pieces that balance one another but are individually different. Unlike modernism that is defined by the search for objective truth, postmodernism is more defined by a search for equity, an ethical balance symbolized by the collage.

But the focus on the search in both periods speaks to the lack of an epistemological foundation, which had been provided by Christian faith. An artist can simply paint what is seen, but who is to say that it is not an illusion? (Schaefer 2005, 199)

Is the Modern Era Over?

Placher (1989, 26) starts his discussion of the Enlightenment with the father of the movement, René Descartes, writing:

> Descartes had set the goal of seeking a foundation for knowledge, but modern philosophy soon divided between empiricists who looked for that foundation in bare, uninterrupted sensations [things you see, hear, feel, taste…] and rationalists who sought it in logically unchallengeable first truths.

For empiricists, a problem quickly emerged because:

> We cannot build knowledge on a foundation of uninterpreted sense-data, because we cannot know particular sense-data in isolation from the

conceptual schemes we use to organize them. (Placher 1989, 29)

If this point is not obvious, think about how we know that a light is red and different from yellow or green. The difference hangs on the definition of red and how it differs from yellow or green. Without knowing that definition, red is not a distinct color. We teach colors to children at a young age, so they seem obvious to us as adults, but to untaught kids, the color differences are arbitrary. The definition of red is a conceptual scheme.

For logicians, Placher (1989, 33) observes:

> What we cannot do is find some point that is uniquely certain by definition, guarantee to hold regardless of any empirical discoveries, independent of any other elements in the our system.

Placher (1989, 32) notes the definition of a mammal, *"a warm-blooded animal with hair which bears live young,"* had to change with the discovery of the platypus, a mammal that lays eggs. While the platypus problem seems trivial, Placher (1989, 34) notes that:

> If our definitions in mathematics or logic lead to problems, we may decide to change them, but we always have more than one choice [of definition].

In conclusion, Placher (1989, 34) cites Wittgenstein observing:

> when we find the foundations, it turns out they

are being held up by the rest of the house. If theologians try to defend their claims by starting with basic, foundational truths that any rational person would have to believe or observations independent of theory and assumptions, they are trying to do something that our best philosophers tell us is impossible.

In other words, Enlightenment scholars have failed to find a philosophically defensible basis for objective truth.

A Picture of Postmodernism From Modeling

Placer argues that the idea of objective truth cannot be validated philosophically as a logical framework. Because belief in objective truth defined the modern period, the absence of validation marked the beginning of the postmodern era.[1] Let me offer an illustration from economic modeling.

The typical argument in economics is metaphorical— for example, we can characterize the economy as aggregate demand defined as the sum of consumption, investment, and government spending. To perform a mental experiment, we might change government spending while holding consumption and investment constant. The effect on aggregate demand is accordingly limited to the effect of the change in government spending. The size of the effect will be determined by statistical estimates of past aggregate demand.

This type of modeling is referred to as a static equilibrium model because we make our forecasts based on one variable changing at a time. This is a linear argument familiar to economists trained in the modern period. What changed in the postmodern period was the idea of allowing all the variables to change simultaneously—the introduction of general equilibrium models. Mathematically, these models could only be approximated, not statistically estimated in the prior sense. General equilibrium models are indeterminate, having no fixed solution because the solution depends on the starting point assumed—a completely arbitrary assumption. Even the coefficients of the equation can vary (Swamy 1971).

The reason for this intractability arises because the historical experience likely does not offer observations on changes that might be expected in the future. In the 1980s, for example, we saw interest rates rise to levels not previously seen. The Great Recession, likewise, saw housing prices fall further than ever previously observed.

Postmodern Dilemma

This hypothetical modeling complexity is precisely the same problem faced by postmodern society—too many cultural norms have been altered too quickly. With the traditional sources of personal stability—family, work, church, education, technology, attitudes about gender, authority, freedom—in motion, we observe high levels of anxiety, depression, and suicide (Bernstein 2018). In this context of instability, we hear professionals telling stories about how a complex cultural system will evolve in response to changes never previous experienced and outside their own area of expertise (Hart 2009, 3–4).

In his work on scientific paradigm shifts, for example, Kuhn (1996, 7) writes:

> A new theory, however special its range of application, is seldom or never just an increment to what is already known. Its assimilation requires the reconstruction of prior theory [a story or metaphor of how things work] and the re-evaluation of prior fact, an intrinsically revolutionary process that is seldom completed by a single man and never overnight. No wonder historians have had difficulty in dating [these changes] precisely this extended process that their vocabulary impels them to view as an isolated event.

The older, more gratifying process of imaging one change at a time no longer appears tractable. The role of Christian apologetics is to make sense of the new environment and how the Christian message can lead us, our kids, and our neighbors back to God.

The Story Criteria

*N*o proof of God's existence can logically be given. This does not mean that we have no evidence of God's existence or that we should resign ourselves to the big gulp theory of faith, which implies that everything must simply be taken on faith, as if memorizing a confessional statement were sufficient.

Evidence of God's Work in the World

The Bible talks extensively about truth. Jesus describes the Holy Spirit as the Spirit of Truth (John 14:17), and Peter calls the Gospel the Way of Truth (2 Pet 2:2). Furthermore, John testifies as an eyewitness to the truth of the Gospel (1 John 1:1–3). Later, we read:

> We are from God. Whoever knows God listens to us; whoever is not from God does not listen to us. By this we know the Spirit of truth and the spirit of error. Beloved, let us love one another, for love is from God, and whoever loves has been born of God and knows God. Anyone who does not love does not know God, because God is love. (1 John 4:6–8)

Here, the Apostle John sees love as evidence of God's existence and revelation to us. While the postmodern pre-occupation with love may be unhelpful because of the many false definitions of love given, John does two interesting things in this passage.

First, John assumes that the presence of God can be

observed in people. This implies that, although proof of God's existence cannot be logically proved, we still have evidence.

Second, this evidence of God's existence is relational. Love requires an object; it does not stand alone.

Choose a Model

The finances of highly complex companies are typically modeled to advise managers because financial contracts contain option provisions that depend on unknown future circumstances. Even a simple home mortgage, for example, may allow the purchaser to prepay their loan or may contain a variable rate provision that determines the interest rate paid based on changes in market rates.

The reason for these models is simple: the companies are too complex and market transactions take place too quickly to manage them by rule of thumb. To manage a financial corporation without a model would spell disaster in a fast-paced market. Consequently, the criteria for evaluating any particular model is simple: Will a new model perform better than the old one? In some sense, this criterion is a restatement of simple hypothesis testing—does the evidence support the primary or the secondary hypothesis better?

Criteria for Faith

From statistical theory, we know that observations can be classified into schemas (or forms) to measure changes and describe patterns that may, in turn, suggest hypotheses (Placher 1989, 29). In formal research, we test our hypotheses to see which one better explains the patterns in data that we observe.

Observations to Confirm or Reject an Hypothesis

Just like a large corporation, in our complex, ever-changing world, we experience and observe things (our data) that may (or may not) point to God. We can tell stories about how this complicated world works (our hypotheses) that can be used either to point to God—or not.

The criterion for faith then becomes: Is the Christian story about God more credible than alternative stories about how the world works? Hart (2009, ix) writes:

> It may be impossible to provide perfectly irrefutable evidence for one's conclusions, but it is certainly possible to amass evidence sufficient to confirm them beyond plausible doubt.

In this paradigm, the criteria for faith is nothing more than a simplified version of the scientific method. Is it any wonder then that many Christians work in science and find their faith perfectly compatible with their training and experience?

Applying the Criteria

Is the Gospel story better than alternative views of the world?

Frequently when people want to argue that the answer is no, they focus on individual autonomy over family and community, and neglect to consider the entire human condition, from birth to death. The case for abortion, for example, was argued in terms of the right of women to choose rather than the right of the fetus to live. Implications of abortion for families, population growth, and immigration have not received much attention in the public debate in recent years.

The usual answer is yes. The Christian story about God is not only the most credible story about how the world works, but it is also the most desirable. An illustration starts with the creation account where God creates Adam and Eve together in his own image (Gen 1:27). As Hoekema (1994, 97) observes: *"Man is not the image of God by himself, and the woman cannot be the image of God by herself."* Equal rights were not an act of Congress or a judgment handed down by the Supreme Court. God conferred equal rights in creation.

Being created in the image of God, even if tarnished by sin, is the heart of the dignity of all human beings. The Apostle Paul said it best: *"There is neither Jew nor Greek, there is neither slave nor free, there is no male and female, for you are all one in Christ Jesus."* (Gal 3:28) Human rights begin when we realize that we are created in God's image, irrespective of ethnicity, class, or gender.

Resilience of the Gospel

*T*he history of Christian conversions includes a surprising number of staunch critics of the Gospel who, after examining the biblical evidence, admitted their errors and professed faith in Christ. Even though each conversion experience is unique, these critics often deliberated for many years. If the criteria for accepting evidence in the postmodern era focuses on who tells the better story, then these conversion stories provide evidence that the Gospel is indeed one of the best stories around.

The Apostle Paul

The pattern set by the Apostle Paul is emblematic. The Book of Acts introduces Paul, formerly a devout and highly educated Jew known as Saul, as a key instigator in the stoning death of Stephen (Acts 7:58). As a prosecutor of Christian converts from Judaism, we can surmise that the only Christians witnesses to Saul were those he dragged off to prison (Acts 8:3). And Saul was not just another prosecutor, he was infamous among disciples, as we read:

> But Saul, still breathing threats and murder against the disciples of the Lord, went to the high priest and asked him for letters to the synagogues at Damascus, so that if he found any belonging to the Way, men or women, he might bring them bound to Jerusalem. (Acts 9:1–2)

But even this prosecutor was not beyond salvation. On the road to Damascus, Saul met the risen Christ and was left blinded by the experience. He was then led by hand to Damascus, where he refused to eat or drink anything for three days. On the third day, God appeared to a disciple named Ananias and instructed him to visit Saul. Knowing Saul's reputation, Ananias objected. Nevertheless, Ananias visited Saul, healed his blindness, and baptized him. Within days, Paul began preaching that Jesus is the Son of God in the synagogues, and learned that his former colleagues among the Jews were plotting to kill him. Paul escaped Damascus by being lowered at night over the city walls in a basket (Acts 9:3–24).

Paul's conversion changed his life from chief prosecutor to Christian evangelist within a couple weeks. Paul's conversion story made a big impression on the church, which we know because the author of the Book of Acts, Luke, repeated the story three times (Acts 9, 22, 26), and because many Christians never got over their fear of Paul because of his role in persecuting the church (Acts 9:26).

Saint Augustine

Augustine of Hippo (354–430 AD) began life as the son of a wealthy pagan and a Christian mother. Fond of partying, sexual immorality, and keeping questionable company, he had a son by a concubine and confessed to robbing a neighbor's orchard just for kicks and giggles. Unsettled by the depth of his sin at the age of thirty-two, Augustine confessed to God in private, as he reported:

> Such things I said, weeping in the most bitter sorrow of my heart. And suddenly I hear a voice from some nearby house, a boy's voice or a girl's voice, I do not know, but it was a sort of sing-song, repeated again and again, Take and read, take and read. (Foley 2006, 169)

Augustine borrowed a book of scripture from his friend, Alypius, and opened it randomly coming to this verse:

> Let us walk properly as in the daytime, not in orgies and drunkenness, not in sexual immorality and sensuality, not in quarreling and jealousy. (Rom 13:13)

Convicted of his own sexual sin, he took this passage as a word from God to him personally and went to his mother to announce that he was a Christian (Foley 2006, 160).

Hounds of Heaven

Having lost his mother at an early age and being dispatched to various, questionable boarding schools by his father, C.S. Lewis became a bitter, young, philosophical atheist. Nevertheless, Lewis writes using different metaphors about God's pursuit of his soul, such as:

> But, of course, what mattered most of all was my deep-seated hatred of authority, my monstrous individualism, my lawlessness. No word in my vocabulary expressed deeper hatred than the word *interference*. But Christianity placed at the center what then seemed to me a transcendental interference. This is my business and mine only. (Lewis 1955, 172)

and *"so the great Angler played His fish and I never dreamed that the hook was in my tongue."* (Lewis 1955, 211)

But for Lewis, the metaphor that he highlights most often is that of a divine chess master in two separate chapter titles: check and checkmate (Lewis 1955, 165, 212). What metaphor would appeal to a scholar and intellectual? Lewis writes of returning to faith in 1929, when he was thirty-one years old (Lewis 1955, 228).

Deep Stocktaking

The template for these conversions is often hostility to the Gospel, deep study of it, and a final ah-ha moment—often unexpected—when the decision for faith takes place. Consider these three other conversions.

First, one Iranian reported being visited by the living Christ while in a coma following a car accident. On waking, she spoke to her father, a Muslim cleric, about being visited by the

Prophet Jesus,[1] but he rebuked her saying that the Prophet could not have visited her because he was dead. Later, she sought out a church because she had never even spoken to a Christian. She married a Christian evangelist, who was martyred for the faith in 1994 (WWM 2014).

Second, consider the story of an atheist journalist with the *Chicago Tribune* named Lee Strobel (2016). After learning that his wife had become a Christian, Strobel set out to prove Christianity was a hoax and to write about it. After considering all the evidence that he assembled, he admitted his mistake, and became not only a believer, but also an evangelist and pastor. Strobel's conversion was made into a movie: *The Case for Christ* (2017).

Third, Rosaria Butterfield (2012, 12–26) was a university professor, a leader among lesbian feminists, and a researcher in queer theory. Determined to write a paper attacking the Christian Right, she researched Christianity by reading the entire New Testament, *Calvin's Institutes*, studying New Testament Greek, and books like Vanhoozer's *Is there Meaning in this Text?* Through her studies and discussions with a local pastor, Butterfield not only to came to faith, she later married a pastor.

In these three conversion accounts, the journey of faith

was long, hard, and involved deep study of the Gospel.

Role of Scripture

The role of scripture in these conversions has been anticipated in scripture itself. The Apostle Paul writes: *"So faith comes from hearing, and hearing through the word of Christ."* (Rom 10:17) In writing about the role of scripture in spiritual formation, David Currie (2018, 51) writes:

> Spiritual formation is the lifelong, faith-filled process of the Holy Spirit transforming the whole person into the loving likeness of Christ to the glory of the Father as informed by the whole word of God, in relationship with the whole people of God to fulfill the whole mission of God.

As in the creation account, *"The Word gives form to what was formless and fills up what was empty."* (Currie 2018, 52) This truth was, of course, the testimony of the Apostle John in his prologue (John 1:1–17). While spiritual direction often plays a role in some of these conversion stories, the scripture itself is sometimes the only path to faith.

Pascal's Wager

The fear of the LORD is the beginning of knowledge;
fools despise wisdom and instruction. (Prov 1:7)

*A*n important atheistic argument for why faith is not rational starts with the observation that the existence of God can neither be logically proven or disproven. Atheists focusing on this observation prefer the term *agnostic* that in Greek means not knowing, suggesting insufficient evidence for a faith decision.

Contrary to the definition of agnostic, the agnostic is not a neutral observer. Every human being has a set of priorities in which the first priority defines how the rest are interpreted. The number-one priority is often to remain in control of one's own life; alternatively, it is a spouse or other person or something like work.

Personal Crisis

As a young person, I experience a crisis of faith when the elders of the church dismissed my youth director in my junior year in high school. This youth director had encouraged me to take an active role in the youth group and to take my faith seriously. When she left the church, I bitterly resented her dismissal and became angry at God. My experience with the church had posed an important barrier to faith as a young adult.

Even in my absence from the church and bitterness at God, I felt his presence. After about three years, I realized that the bitterness was directed at the leadership of the church who had dismissed my youth director, not at God. Sorting out my own anger permitted me to reconsider faith, and I sought a new church.

Pascal's Wager

During my period of anger with God, atheistic arguments never seemed real to me, even when I repeated them, because I knew God firsthand, and I knew that I had been blessed when I came to faith. Pascal's Wager, which was directed at atheists, made perfect sense to me, even when I had turned my back on God.

Pascal used probability theory to argue that the agnostic argument is logically false in that faith is a fair bet. If God exists and you believe, then you win heaven, but if God does not exist, you loose nothing.[1] In other words, faith in God has a positive reward provided the probability of God existing is a positive, non-zero number. Betting that God exists is accordingly offers better odds than organized gambling, where the house normally earns a substantial profit, suggesting that the odds in betting are negative—not a fair bet.

Going back to the agnostic's assertion that the evidence

for God is inconclusive, Pascal's wager breaks the tie in being a fair bet. In addition, living as if God exists provides meaning to life, peace with God, and fellowship with the church, all net benefits. For example, researchers at Duke University (1999) reported:

> A study of nearly 4,000 elderly North Carolinians has found that those who attended religious services every week were 46 percent[2] less likely to die over a six-year period than people who attended less often or not at all, according to researchers at Duke University Medical Center.[3]

Ignoring these benefits accordingly reveals that the agnostic holds a bias against faith.

Arguments for God's Existence

A core tenet of the scientific method lies in using reproducible empirical evidence to validate or fail to validate a hypothesis. Clark (2001, 3) writes:

> Evidentialism maintains that a belief is rational for a person only if that person has sufficient evidence or arguments or reasons for that belief.

Because God created the heavens and the earth, he lies outside the created order, where direct evidence might be found. Therefore, scientific testing of the existence (or nonexistence) of God is impossible, as evidentialists have argued. However, we can infer the existence of God from the created order, much like we might observe fingerprints of a potter on the pottery—a kind of indirect evidence.[1]

Introduction

In his recent book, *Making Sense of God*, Timothy Keller (2016, 217) summarizes six arguments for the existence of God from: existence, fine tuning, moral realism, consciousness, reason, and beauty[2] that bear repeating.

From Existence

For existence to even be, it required an uncaused cause (Keller 2016, 218).[3] Think about the evolutionary hypothesis that posits that life spontaneously emerged from non-biological substances and evolved until the creation of human beings. But who created the non-biological substances? The usual response is that the universe just always existed. However, according to the Big Bang theory, the universe has not always looked like it does today.

According to one online dictionary[4] the Big Bang theory is:

> a theory in astronomy: the universe originated billions of years ago in an explosion from a single point of nearly infinite energy density.

Given that the universe shows evidence of an uncaused cause, it is reasonable to infer that God created the universe in his own inscrutable way.

From Fine Tuning

Constants in physics appear to be precisely adjusted to allow life to exist. Keller (2016, 219) writes:

> The speed of light, the gravitational constant, the strength of the strong and weak nuclear forces— must all have almost exactly the values that they do have in order for organic life to exist…the chances that all of the dials would be tuned to life-permitting settings all at once are about 10^{-100}.

Given the small probability that the laws of physics randomly aligned in this way, many scientists have concluded that the universe was intentionally designed, an argument first attributed to William Paley (1743–1805). It is like finding a working clock on the beach—no reasonable person would assume that this clock was randomly created. The existence of a clock suggests a clock maker.

An interesting example of this fine-tuning came up in NOVA's 2017 show *The Day the Dinosaurs Died*, a day some 66 million years ago. Scientists believe that a seven-mile across asteroid collided with earth off the coast of Mexico to create the Chicxulub crater. Worldwide extinctions followed primarily because the asteroid's impact vaporized large quantities of gypsum found in that particular area that rained down on the dinosaurs both on land and in the sea in the form of sulfuric acid. Had the meteor landed seconds earlier or later, because of the speed of the asteroid and the earth rotation, it would have landed in the Atlantic or Pacific oceans and caused only local damage, not global extinctions. Had the dinosaurs survived, mammals, like humans, would likely not have evolved into the dominant species.[5]

David Hume (1711–1776), argued that the universe is unique, and therefore any discussion about its origin is anthropomorphic (speculative) or simply an analogy. Charles Darwin (1809–1882) believed that his theory of evolution explained the complexity found in the biological world (Clark

2001, 28–34).[6] However, the argument from design continues to bring the most scientists to faith.

From Moral Realism

Most people, even ardent atheists, believe that moral obligations, like human rights, exist that we can insist everyone abide by. Keller (2016, 221) writes:

> Some things are absolutely wrong to do. Moral obligation, then, makes more sense in a universe created by a personal God to whom we intuitively feel responsible than it does in an impersonal universe with no God.

Even an ardent atheist would not idly stand by and watch another person drown or die helplessly in a burning house when something could be done to aid them. This kind of moral obligation is something virtually everyone feels, yet is counter-intuitive from the perspective of personal survival—water rescues and running into burning buildings routinely kill rescuers, even those trained as lifeguards and firefighters. Why do we feel obligated to put ourselves at such risk? Christians answer that God created us with a moral compass.

From Consciousness

Keller (2016, 222), citing Thomas Nagel (2012, 110), writes that *"all human experience has a subjective quality to it."* It is pretty hard to argue, as does Francis Crisk (1994, 3), that

You, your joys and your sorrows, your memories and ambitions, your sense of personal identity and free will, are in fact no more than the behavior of a vast assembly of nerve cells and their associated molecules. (Keller 2016, 224)

Keller (2016, 224) summarizes: *"Consciousness and idea making make far more sense in a universe created by an idea-making, conscious God."*

From Reason and Beauty

Keller (2016, 225) reports that has been popular in recent years to argue that our reasoning and appreciation of beauty both developed from the process of natural selection because they helped our ancestors to survive. Evolutionary psychologists have gone a step further, arguing that even our faith in God is a product of evolution and natural selection.

The problem exists, however, that many animals seem to have survived just fine without developing any capacity to reason at all. Furthermore, if our faith is a product of natural selection, why wouldn't we trust our reasoning capacity to tell us the truth? The arguments for beauty parallel those for reason.

Keller (2016, 226), citing Luc Ferry (2011), writes: *"truth, beauty, justice, and love ... whatever the materialists say, remain fundamentally transcendent"* because they all point to the existence of a loving God.

Limits to the Proofs

Most proofs of God's existence make it sensible to believe in God in an abstract or philosophical sense. They really do not give us a detailed picture of God's character, as revealed in the Bible.

Philosophers remind us that God transcends our universe because he created it—God stands outside time and space. He is also holy—sacred and set apart. God's transcendence makes it impossible for us to approach God on our own; he must initiate any contact that we have with him. Christians believe that God revealed himself to us in the person of Jesus Christ.

The Uniqueness of Christ

The death and resurrection of Jesus Christ makes the case that God not only exists, but that he is God of the Old and New Testaments. Keller (2016, 228) observes that only Christianity is truly a world religion; it has had indigenous believers fairly evenly distributed across all regions and continents of the world, long before it became a religion in Europe and North America. He writes: *"today most of the most vital and largest Christian populations are now nonwhite and non-Western."*

The arguments for God's existence must be compelling (or Christians must have come to faith for other reasons) because Christianity continues to grow in spite of strong influence of secularism in the West and obvious persecution of Christians outside the West.

Arguments About Creation

*D*iscussions about the rationality of faith in the twentieth century invariably focus on the Genesis account of creation: its biblical interpretation, the Darwin discoveries, and the political context. Let me consider each in turn.

What Does Genesis Say?

The first chapter in Genesis paints a picture of God as divine creator who calls the universe into being with words spoken over a period of seven days. While much is made of God as a sovereign, king of kings, the language here is not one of command, but of invitation: *"Let there be."* God is a gentle sovereign who rules by virtue of creative activity, not conquest nor purchase, nor chance. In his first specific act of creation, God created light—a metaphor for virtue (Gen 1:3).

The first verse offers a summary: *"In the beginning, God created the heavens and the earth."* (Gen. 1:1) This one verse radically changed the perception of time and space. In the Ancient Near East, the time that mattered was day and night, and the seasons—spring, summer, fall, and winter—that controlled the cycles of agriculture. The space that mattered was the boundaries on a particular kingdom or empire. Here in this verse, God stands outside of time and space, creating both. There are no paths up the mountain to God, because he transcends both. The God of Genesis must come down the mountain to us.

How Do We Know?

The Genesis account comes to us as the confession of the church. In creating the universe *ex nihilo* (out of nothing), the god in Genesis is nothing like other gods of the Ancient Near East, which appeared more like today's celebrities, political leaders, war heroes, movie stars, and athletes. God redefined what it meant to be a god.

Not only was he sovereign; he was completely free of the constraints of this world. When God told Moses from the burning bush: *"I AM WHO I AM"* (Exod 3:14), what he meant was: I am the real deal—the real God, not like the wish-fulfillment gods that we create to serve our own needs.

The Darwin Discoveries

The nineteenth century brought amazing discoveries about our world in agriculture, manufacturing, science, and medicine. While authors like Marx and Freud likened religion to being on drugs and delusional, Darwin focused on exploring the biological world and taking stock of the fossil record without venturing into politics or religion. Those who came after Darwin were not so circumspect.

Theorizing that ancient species of animals evolved into those that we see today, Darwin's theory of evolution quickly became viewed as a competing vision of the creation account in Genesis.

Political Uses of Evolution

From the spontaneous generation of life from inorganic compounds to the development of human species, Darwin gave Marxists and other secular religionists a creation account that erased God from the picture. National Socialists in Germany picked up on Darwin's survival of the fittest to posit the existence of a master race, the German folk.[1] The attacks on the creation accounts in Genesis elevated quickly into power politics on a world scale. If *"God is dead"* as Nietzsche philosophized in Also Sprach Zarathustra, then *"everything is permitted,"* opined Dostoyevsky in *The Brothers Karamazov.*

Shafer-Landau (2018, 66–67) cites the Dostoyevsky reference in exploring the implications of divine command theory, which states: *"An act is morally required just because it is commanded by God, and immoral just because God forbids it."* Philosophers since Plato have argued that the gods command morality because it makes sense, not as an arbitrary command. Thus, the liberty that many feel disparaging God's existence is misplaced, because morality has its own logic.

After Nietzsche, atheistic political groups, such as the National Socialists in Germany and the communists elsewhere, felt at liberty in the twentieth century to ignore human rights, and to imprison and murder their opponents. Schaeffer (2005, 151) writes:

> Heinrich Himmler (1900–1945), leader of the Gestapo, stated that the law of nature must take its course in the survival of the fittest. The result was the gas chambers. Hitler states numerous times that Christianity and its notion of charity should be 'replaced by the ethic of strength over weakness.'

Millions perished when Hitler applied Darwin's theories in service to his prejudices. Millions more perished in Soviet gulags.[2]

Returning to Genesis

God's invitation in creation does not describe how the universe was created, only who created it. Borrowing a legal analogy, when Congress passes a law, it usually does not care how the President implements the law beyond offering resources and perhaps a target deadline. God could easily have used evolution to create life as we know it.

A Doubting Church

The problem in the nineteenth century arose as doubt in society seeped into the church. Some found refuge in philosophic defenses of God's existence, while others labored to make sure that Christians experienced deep emotional experiences in the pews on Sunday through great music and a good sermon. Rather than calling out Marx and Freud for slandering God and his church, many took them seriously and even expanded on what had been said.

One example of such influence came in criticism of the Book of Genesis. Motivated by anti-Semitic views, some nineteenth century German authors tried to sift out the Jewish influence on Genesis, known as the priestly source in the Documentation Hypothesis, and to attack the authorship of Moses (Blenkinsopp 1992, 11–13).

The Documentation Hypothesis was later discredited for its arbitrary division of Genesis into various pieces, but the greater damage to scholarship came in leading people to question the divine inspiration of scripture and the authorship of Moses. Among some academic circles, the Bible became just another book worthy perhaps of historical interest and study, but no longer treated as authoritative for the church.

Science in Service of Faith

The fascination with science peaked during World War II. With the invention of numerous instruments of mass destruction—bombings, napalm, death camps, nuclear weapons, and political uses of psychology and euthanasia—people woke up to the need for limits on scientific investigation.

Several aspects of science proved helpful in understanding our faith. One is to notice that the scientific method—felt need, problem definition, data collection, analysis, recommendations, responsibility bearing—starts with assumptions about what is needed. These assumptions about how our world works start with the words we use and our faith.

The Big Bang theory of creation started from measurement of the direction and speed of partials in space that point to a particular time and place where the known universe began with a singularity—a single point. In an instant, the entire universe came into being.

Is the Genesis creation account consistency with the Big Bang theory an accident or is it another example of how the Bible is simply the best story around?

Postmodernism

*I*n his book, *Who's Afraid of Postmodernism*, James Smith (2006, 26) describes post modernism as an historical period after (post) modernism, heavily influenced by French philosophers, especially Jacques Derrida, Jean-François Lyotard, and Michael Foucault. Smith observes that postmodernism does not make a clean break with modernism, but tends to intensify certain aspects of modernism, particularly notions of freedom (Smith 2006, 19–21, 26).

Smith argues that these three postmodern philosophers have been misunderstood and are compatible with the traditional teaching of the church when properly understood. The collapse of the church in our lifetime can accordingly be seen to lay the groundwork for a revitalization of the church around traditional teaching, once purged of its modernistic thought patterns (Smith 2006, 22–23, 29).

Jacques Derrida

Smith's premise is that these philosophers have been misunderstood because of the weak summaries given of them. For example, Derrida's misunderstood statement is: *"There is nothing outside the text."* (Smith 2006, 36) The idea that one can simply read a text, particularly an ancient text written in another language, and understand its meaning is to misunderstand the role of language, context, and interpretation.

While often said to mean that the Bible cannot be read and understood by just anyone, Smith says that this is not what Derrida is saying. Derrida's point is simply that all texts require interpretation, which implies that objective truth is unattainable (Smith 2006, 38–40, 43).

Jean-François Lyotard

Smith also sees Lyotard's idea of a meta-narrative as misunderstood. Postmodern critics have trouble with the meta-narrative or big story of scripture—creation, fall, redemption, and eschatology. Smith sees Lyotard's main concern is not with the church but the truth claims of modern science. Science is itself a meta-narrative that falsely and deceptively claims to be universal, objective, and demonstrable through reason alone. Smith writes: *"For the postmodern, every scientist is a believer."* Lyotard is perfectly okay with the idea of faith preceding reason, following Augustine (Smith 2006, 62–72) and Anselm, who wrote: *"I believe so that I may understand."* (Davies and Evans 2008, 87)

Michael Foucault

Foucault's concern about institutional power structures is hard to summarize because he resists reductionism in his writing style and focuses on tediously pure description. Smith sees Foucault preoccupied with disciplinary structures, but wonders what his real intentions are. Smith (2006, 102) writes:

> What is wrong with all these disciplinary structures is not that they are bent on forming or molding human beings into something, but rather what they are aiming for in that process.

Smith sees Foucault offering three lessons to the church. They are to see *"how pervasive disciplinary formation is within our culture;"* to identify which of these disciplines are *"fundamentally inconsistent with…the message of the church;"* and to *"enact countermeasures, counter disciplines that will form us into the kinds of people that God calls us to be"* (Smith 2006, 105–106).

Weakness in Modern Witness

Smith sees hope in the Derrida's critique because the modern understanding of the Christian message is itself a distortion of traditional church teaching. In framing the Christian message in ahistorical truth statements (God is love; 1 John 3:8), the narrative tradition (God showed his love by sending his son into the world; John 3:16–17) has been lost and the church has found itself unable to retain the moral context of the biblical accounts.

Because the Christian message is contextual in

biblical accounts and is interpreted by the church, it meets Derrida's primary concerns. The church must, therefore, abandon modern thought and language in order to thrive in the postmodern environment (Smith 2006, 54–58).

IMPLICATIONS

Overview

*T*he Western church's inadequate response to modernism has hastened the demise of Christendom and made the philosophical transition from modernism to postmodernism more obvious. Modernism prompted a backing away from the narrative of scripture and the embracing of a conceptual, individualistic, and private approach to the Gospel. This facilitated a spilling over of Greek dualism from society into the theology of the church and weakened its witness in an artificial division between emotional worship and rational apologetics.

Moving from the modern to the postmodern era changes how we explain the Gospel, closing some doors and opening others. While cultural Christianity is sterile and cannot reproduce itself, God's will cannot help but be accomplished.

Many of the critiques of faith and postmodern culture highlight or allege a lack of proper mental function or a deviation from rationality. In this final chapter, I look at some of the postmodern challenges and talk about some of the opportunities. Because faith is not optional, the question is not faith or no faith, but finding faith in God.

God is my Denominator

*T*he postmodern era is rife with religious alternatives. In my hometown of Centreville, Virginia, we have several Hindu temples, Mosques, and, being near Washington DC, many secular people. Still, most Americans identify themselves as Christians.

Changing Christian Identity

Three out of four Americans have some Christian background, but only two in five Christians actively practice their faith. The good news is that the share of Christians who practice their faith has remained relatively stable over the generations. The bad news is that the declining share of nominal Christians has hastened the demise of Christendom and dominates the headlines (Kinnamen and Lyon 2016, 27, 224).

Role of Faith

While most discussions of faith focus on its content and outward practice, it is helpful to view faith in terms of priorities. Citing Bruce Leafbald,[1] Giglio (2003, 117) defines true worship as *"centering our mind's attention and our heart's affection on the Lord."* What do we really worship? Giglio (2003, 13) writes: *"follow the trail of your time, your affection, your energy, your money, and your loyalty ... [that] is what you [really] worship."*

As the First Commandment reads: *"You shall have no other gods before me."* (Exod 20:3)

If God is truly the first priority in your life, your faith becomes the denominator against which all other activities in life are measured. Blamires (2005, 44) writes:

> To think Christianly is to accept all things with the mind as related, directly or indirectly, to man's eternal destiny as the redeemed and chosen child of God.

In money terms, it's like the gold standard of the nineteenth century—all prices were measured in terms of the amount of gold required to make a purchase. Or, following Gödel's *Incompleteness Theorem* cited earlier, God is the assumption taken from outside our closed world that offers stability to our lives (Smith 2001, 89). By contrast, if God is just one of many priorities, you are at risk of falling into idolatry.

Idolatry as a False Priority

The Bible pictures idols as graven images or statutes (Ps 115:3–8). But this statuesque view of idolatry is less helpful than to view idolatry as misplaced priorities. If something other than God is our first priority, then it is like trying to do business with counterfeit money—you may be able to fool a few people, but pretty soon it will catch up to you. Idols let us down hard when they invariably break, as discussed previously.

Today's Spiritual Crisis

The spiritual wanderlust that America is experiencing today starts with misplaced priorities that creates a spiritual vacuum, which may be filled by many substitutes—syncretistic Christianity, alternative religions, and addictions, especially idolatry. But because we are created in the image of God (Gen 1:27), these idols cannot bring the peace that only God bring.

The Pathological Culture

*L*et's return to a question posed earlier. What if a culture evolved that, far from supporting and sustaining proper function, made proper function more costly and unlikely? Would we see more dysfunction, anxiety, and suicide as people found it harder to survive and thrive?

Proper Mental Function and Rational Culture

If as Plantinga (2000, xi, 153–154) argued proper mental function is a requirement for warranted faith, then it is also required to meet the demands of rationality, which drives our earlier understanding of culture as a deviation from perfect rationality. Much like a traditional, modern, and postmodern cultures are deviations from perfect rationality, one could argue that secular culture is a deviation from perfect Christianity.

The Apostle Paul appears to be focused on this line of thinking when he writes about God's peace:

> Whatever is true, whatever is honorable, whatever is just, whatever is pure, whatever is lovely, whatever is commendable, if there is any excellence, if there is anything worthy of praise, think about these things. (Phil 4:8)

We can infer from Paul's bracketing in verses seven and nine with God's peace that when we take Christ as our role model we become more truthful, honorable, pure, lovely, and commendable.

I could see Plantinga adding *"more rational"* to Paul's list.

A Breakdown in Authority

If God is no longer a transcendent reality for most people, then leaders in society no longer feel accountable for their actions outside of a political context. If postmodern society is also suspicious of all formers of authority (Blamires 2005, 132–133), then our models of proper mental function and perfect rationality should start to show wear and tear.

One explanation for this wear and tear is that the vesting of authority in parents, teachers, preachers, police, and government officials offers coherence and consistency to culture that is mostly dispersed in postmodern culture. Deconstructionism, a postmodern philosophy that is suspicious of all authority figures, disenfranchises traditional and modern leaders, through encouraing lawsuits and frivolous attacks, thus reducing the incentive to invest in leadership roles that previously gave stability to the culture.

A second explanation is that postmodernism no longer shares Christian presuppositions that gave a foundation to objective truth during the modern era. Most moderns grew up in at least a nominally Christian environment, much like Nietzsche, who was the son of a Lutheran pastor. Even if they rejected Christian faith, they knew its foundations. By contrast, many postmoderns are like sons of Nietzsche, who have little or no experience with Christian beliefs, and, because of the hermeneutics of suspicion,[1] are not open to learning about it.

A third explanation is that postmodern culture's emphasis on diversity is appealing, but, unlike objective truth, does not provide a firm organizing principle. For example, how does a foundation choose among various diseases to invest research money? An objective answer might be to fund research for the disease with the highest mortality rate, something easily determined.

In a postmodern context, the answer is inherently political, forcing the question to morph into what is the disease that would be most popular to cure? Because a consensus view is unlikely, the decision also would have to consider who might protest if their favorite disease is not funded? Clearly, no stable answer to the question can be offered because postmodern culture encourages tribalism that devolves from consensus, rather than converging on it.

Thus, both practical and theoretical reasons can be cited for why postmodernism does not provide a stable foundation for unified, national culture. Instead, it tends to decay into the formation of subcultures (tribes) that pursue their own interests at the expense of the larger society.

Formation in the Home

Consider the problem of raising children. Research by Stinnett and Beam (1999, 10) reports six characteristics of strong families:

> 1. Commitment—these families promote each other's welfare and happiness and value unity.
>
> 2. Appreciation and Affection—strong families care about each other.
>
> 3. Positive Communication—strong families communicate well and spend a lot of time doing it together.
>
> 4. Time Together—Strong families spend a lot of quality time together.
>
> 5. Spiritual Well-being—whether or not they attend religious services, strong families have a sense of a greater good or power in life.
>
> 6. Ability to Cope With Stress and Crisis—strong families see crises as a growth opportunity.

What happens when both spouses work, neither feels like they are in charge, and the family finds itself under economic and time pressure? The strong family model outlined above breaks down. Assuming a strong family starting out, stress shows up potentially in all six characteristics outlined as time and economic pressure are increased.

A key point in unifying these different models of behavior

as it pertains to raising children is that adults are present and fully attentive to the children. When television becomes the primary baby-sitter, and the adults are buzzing to and from work and activities for the children, the children are not formed rationally or becoming more Christlike. The model of strong families clearly is being tested severely in our society.

Signs of Wear and Tear

News reports and studies showing a stagnating standard of living, drug use, declining fertility rates, lower life expectancy levels, and record levels of suicide all point to a culture under stress.[2] This stress leads to greater deviations from rationality because highly rational decisions require time and energy that are no longer available.

Citing Edward Gibbon's classic book, *Decline and Fall of the Roman Empire* (1776–1788), Schaeffer (2005, 227) lists five indicators of Rome's decline:

1. A mounting love of show and luxury,

2. A widening gap between rich and poor,

3. An obsession with sex,

4. Freakishness in the arts, and

5. An increasing desire to live off the state.

Today we have a president famous for his luxurious lifestyle; an economy primarily benefitting the wealthy; celebrities flaunting their sexuality; music and the arts appearing incomprehensible; and a federal government massively in debt because of military spending, social welfare programs, tax cuts, and corporate largesse. The comparison with the late Roman Empire seems apropos.

In this environment, we expect cultural change to occur more rapidly and to morph over time into a traditional culture.

The Broken Glass Theory

While the exact time-path and particular difficulties cannot be exactly forecasted, the general trends are obvious. Dysfunction in one area of society increases the likelihood of contagion elsewhere. In his book, *Serious Times*, James Emory White (2004, 158) highlights of the broken glass theory of criminologists James O. Wilson and George Kelling (1982). The idea is that crime is contagious. It starts with a broken window, and spreads with greater crime throughout an entire community.

By cleaning up trash, graffiti, and broken windows and minor violations of law through increased emphasis on foot patrols by police, New York City substantially reduced crime in the 1980s. For those of us who grew up scared to walk the streets of New York, this reduction in crime was a big deal. Pushback against this program came later, as not everyone was happy about the increased police presence in the neighborhoods. As predicted earlier, cultures under stress tend to revert to traditional cultural attributes, as we see here in the re-introduction of street cops in New York City.

Small things matter, which gives the broken glass theory a familiar ring: *"I am the LORD who brought you up out of Egypt to be your God; therefore be holy, because I am holy."* (Lev 11:45). If attending to the appearance of neighborhoods in New York helped reduce crime, how much more could focusing on Christ's model improve the quality of life in our families, churches, and communities?

The Church as an Authority

$\mathcal{E}$ arlier we saw how the important authorities are in our decisions. Each Christian has Christ as a mentor, but we also have human mentors within our families, church, and community. Because I have talked already about the transition from a modern to a postmodern culture, let me turn to discuss the church context from my own personal experience.

Upbringing in the Church

The Hiemstra family has over the past hundred years been associated with the Reformed Church in America (RCA), a church associated with the Dutch immigrant communities in New England and the Midwest. I was baptized in an RCA church. My uncle John is a retired RCA pastor, who has been a lifelong mentor. When my family moved to Washington, DC in 1960, no RCA churches could be found within driving distance, so we attended Presbyterian churches in the Presbyterian Church in the United States (PCUSA), where my dad and I both have been ordained as elders. My mother grew up in the Baptist tradition associated with Scotch-Irish communities, but in marriage, she became a Presbyterian.

Denominational Identities

Both the RCA and the PCUSA arise out of the reformed tradition, which has historically focused theologically on confessional faith. Both denominations affirm these confessions:

> *The Apostles' Creed*
>
> *The Nicene Creed*
>
> *The Heidelberg Catechism*

The RCA uniquely affirms these confessions:

> *The Athanasian Creed*
>
> *The Belgic Confession*
>
> *The Canons of Dort*
>
> *The Confession of Belhar*[1]

The PCUSA uniquely affirms these confessions:

> *The Scots Confession*
>
> *The Second Helvetic Confession*
>
> *The Westminster Confession of Faith*
>
> *The Shorter Catechism*
>
> *The Larger Catechism*
>
> *The Theological Declaration of Barmen*
>
> *The Confession of 1967*
>
> *A Brief Statement of Faith– Presbyterian Church (U.S.A.)*[2]

Theologically, the RCA is the more conservative denomination, having little or no change to their confessional statements or polity in the last hundred years, adding only the *Confession of Belhar,* while the PCUSA has amended its polity (the Book of Order) almost routinely every two years, and affirmed three confessions written in the twentieth century (the last three listed). Coming into the twentieth century, the primary confession of churches now affiliated with the PCUSA was the Westminster Confession.

Confessional Wunderlust

It is widely recognized that the RCA takes its identity primarily in its reformed confessions, while the PCUSA's identity is vested in its polity, a twentieth century development.

For more than three hundred years, the *Westminster Confession* united Presbyterians in the Americas. It was written in 1640 and adopted early on as the primarily confessional document among Presbyterians and remains in use today. However, the attitude about the confession changed dramatically in the twentieth century. This confession served first as a bulwark against liberalism in the early part of the century, but in the 1930s, the General Assembly passed a resolution forbidding any part of the denomination from offering an authoritative interpretation of the *Westminster Confession*. Later, a *Book of Confessions* aggregated a number of confessional statements, leaving the *Westminster Confession* simply one of many (Longfield 2013, 15, 126, 142–143, 196).

The Scot's Confession of 1560, which is included in the *Book of Confessions of the Presbyterian Church in the U.S.A.* (PCUSA), outlines three conditions for a true church.[3] A true church is one where the word of God is rightly preached, the sacraments rightly administered, and church discipline rightly administered.

The PCUSA removed its ordination requirements centered on the five fundamentals of the faith in 1925. When it then moved away from the *Westminster Confession* in the next decade, it effectively lost the ability to practice church discipline on the basis of common doctrine and to distinguish itself as a true church as defined in the *Scot Confession*.[4] The boundaries between church and society fuzzed because of doctrinal diversity and with the passage of time the fuzz grew as elected elders and ordained pastors held increasingly diverse views. Thus, Presbyterians transitioned from being a reformed, confessional church to being a church defined primarily by a common polity

.

Ecclesiastical Authority

The authority of the church is vested in scripture and the witness of the Holy Spirit, given on the Day of Pentecost (Acts 2:1–4). The confessions of the church likewise derive their authority from these two sources. When scripture is clear on a subject, the church's role is to teach scripture. When scripture is silent on a subject, the church's role is to interpret scripture under the mentorship of the Holy Spirit. At no point should the church's teaching violate the clear direction of scripture, which is why church discipline is critical to retaining the vitality of the church.

The focus on the authority of scripture has been a distinctive of Protestant churches since the Reformation period of the 1500s, while the Catholic Church has affirmed the authority of tradition in addition to scripture (Sprout 1997, 42–43). The admission of authorities other than scripture, such as tradition, philosophy, and new cultural insights, into Protestant churches represents a return to controversies that led to the first Reformation schism.

In denominations unable or unwilling to maintain church discipline, individual churches are left to themselves in navigating a faithful witness. In churches unable or unwilling to craft a faithful witness, the members themselves must navigate on their own, placing a burden on families to discern for themselves what to believe and how to act on their belief. Consequently, the absence of church discipline has facilitated the rise of individualism within the church.

While God can sovereignly use unfaithful denominations and unfaithful pastors to prosecute his will, we all strive to remain among the faithful at a time when the church is less helpful than it could be in its mentoring role.

The Myth of Perpetual Youth

*T*he phenomena of adulting may seem like a curiosity of postmodern slang, but it is actually at the heart of a powerful shift in American culture that has profound implications for the Christian church. Since the Reagan administration in the 1980s, the American economy has failed to deliver on the American Dream for the majority of citizens (Desilver 2018), prompting a search for a new cultural myth to replace it. Unable to deliver an increasing standard of living for everyone—a nuclear family, house, two cars, healthcare, education, and pension, the *Myth of Perpetual Youth* has increasing been substituted for the American Dream. In effect, advertisers have led the way in declaring: *"Don't worry about not having a spouse, house, car, health plan, education, or pension. Just enjoy being young. Age is just a number."*[1]

The Christian Family

This increased focus on youth stands in opposition to the Gospel.

One of the defining characteristics of the Christian faith is honoring each individual, regardless of age, as being created in the image of God. The Apostle Paul's writing is particularly clear on this point. He writes:

> There is neither Jew nor Greek, there is neither
> slave nor free, there is no male and female, for

you are all one in Christ Jesus. (Gal 3:28)

No ethic group is better than any other; no economic class is better than any other; and no gender is better than any other. Paul goes on to extend his concept to the family:

> Children, obey your parents in the Lord, for this is right. Honor your father and mother (this is the first commandment with a promise), that it may go well with you and that you may live long in the land. Fathers, do not provoke your children to anger, but bring them up in the discipline and instruction of the Lord. (Eph 6:1–4)

Paul is essentially saying that because we are all created in the image of God, no age group is better than any other. Neither a newborn, nor a senior standing at the gates of heaven is better than one another. Christians are to value life stages equally by honoring each stage, and not clinging to any particular stage as if it were intrinsically preferred.

In this sense, Christianity is a holistic faith that values maturity and embraces each stage of life with equal joy. This makes particular sense in a Christian context because our faith is rooted in history. Creation is the beginning and the second coming of Christ will be its end. Knowing the end is in Christ, we can journey through life in Christ meeting the challenges of each stage in life without fear.

The Allure of Youth

The holistic nature of the Christian lifestyle puts it in direct conflict with today's youth culture where putting on a bit of weight or allowing people to see gray hair puts you at risk of being shunned and ridiculed. Celebrities in our culture—politicians, war heroes, athletes, movie stars, musicians, fashion models, the rich—all hide their age judiciously and show as much skin as possible to reinforce the illusion that they remain young. The Christian idea that beauty consists of character and appearance being in sync runs counter to this obsession with appearance (Dyrness 2001, 80).

Ironically, this obsession with youth comes at a time when fewer people are getting married and having children (Pew Research Center 2015). Those that do find less support from families, the church,[2] and even schools for raising healthy kids because the focus has shifted to other age groups.

Think about the holidays. Halloween used to be about little children; now, playing dress up for Halloween has become an obsession for older people. Likewise, the family orientation of Thanksgiving is being eclipsed by retailers anxious to increase winter solstice sales.

Promotion of Inadequacy

While this obsession with youth may seem random, the disfunction of remaining an adolescent well into adulthood and encouraging adolescent attitudes about market purchases may be a direct consequence of strategies employed by advertisers. Inadequacy marketing directly assaults the spirit of most religious teaching, irrespective of theology, because most religions aid our maturation and help us to contribute to society.

Marketing expert Jonah Sacks (2012, 89, 93) writes:

> All story-based marketing campaigns contain an underlying moral of the story and supply a ritual that is suggested to react to that moral.

Inadequacy marketing has two basic steps.

Step one focuses on creating anxiety focusing on an emotion at the base of Maslow's pyramid, which ranks needs from physical needs (base) to emotional needs (top).[3] The advertising moral always begins with *"You are not...and plays off of at least one negative emotion: greed...fear...lust."*

In step two, the ritual proposed is implicitly or explicitly to shop and buy a particular product—pictured as a magical experience. While not all marketers employ inadequacy marketing strategies, the airwaves are inundated with them daily. The same strategies are employed by authors, film-makers, advertisers, religious leaders, and politicians. Advertisers use inadequacy strategies because they work, but an inadvertent result is to encourage fear, anxiety, and a negative self-image particularly among children and those prone to suggestion.

This advertising might be harmless, if it were not repeatedly, endlessly chipping away at our basic morality and promoting a materialistic worldview. Blamires (2005, 74) observes:

> In the world of advertisement no man ever grows older than thirty-five and no woman grows older than twenty-seven. It is a cosy picture of life, full of color and ease. There is always plenty to eat and drink. The furniture never gets old or drab.

While this is less true of advertising today than in the 1960s when Blamires wrote, even the old in advertisements are fitter than most Americans, more fashion aware, and enjoy the active lives of the rich and famous. He observes: *"All around us are advertisements titivating sexual interests, tightening up covetous urges, tantalizing every appetite."* Whenever someone criticizes such things from a Christian perspective, one is treated as out of touch and eccentric (Blamires 2005, 30–31).

Implications

If large corporations find it in their financial interest to keep us feeling inadequate, then the increasing focus on youth in our culture is likely not a random outcome. If significant numbers of people regress to a younger age or never mature beyond a adolescent (teen or preteen) view of the world, what does that imply?

The obvious implication is that an environment is created that mitigates the natural maturation of young people and encourages adolescent attitudes and behaviors. One could speculate that even darker outcomes are possible.

Clearly, much is at stake in encouraging people to follow a normal pattern of maturation rather than getting stuck in a particular stage in life.[4] While answers may be illusive, it is useful to ask: Who benefits from this cultural dysfunction?

The Banality of Evil

And lead us not into temptation,
but deliver us from evil.
(Matt 6:13)

O ne of the greatest challenges in life is the experience of evil, yet in our postmodern world, many people deny its existence, especially the person of Satan. The proclivity to deny evil shows up today in our attempts to define it away. We are not born in sin, as Augustine (Foley 2006, 9) argued; we are born basically good and able to live an righteous life having no need for a savior.

Today when someone points out an obvious sin, the blame is shifted away—the perpetrator was poor, disadvantaged, in great pain, or a victim[1]—a non-liturgical form of the cheap grace that Bonhoeffer (1995, 44–45) warned against. By contrast, the early church routinely practiced exorcism as part of the baptismal service because:

> The exorcisms [meant] to face evil, to acknowledge its reality, to know its power, and to proclaim the power of God to destroy it. (Schmemann 1973, 70–71)

Sin Defined

Sin and evil are birds of a feather. Sin is a broad term encompassing several related ideas: sin, trespass, and iniquity. King David uses all three terms in his prayer of confession over his adultery with Bathsheba:

> Have mercy on me, O God, according to your steadfast love; according to your abundant mercy blot out my transgressions. Wash me thoroughly from my iniquity, and cleanse me from my sin! For I know my transgressions, and my sin is ever before me. (Ps 51:1–3)

In the Greek language, sin is an archery term that means to fall short of the mark. When we strive, but fail, to do good, we sin.

Trespass is a legal term that implies the breaking of a rule or law. Driving at ninety miles per hour on a road with a posted speed limit of fifty-five miles per hour is a trespass.

Iniquity, like sin, can also take a broad meaning but it is helpful to think of iniquity as failing to do something good. The most famous case of the *bystander problem* occurred in New York City (Queens) in 1964 when thirty-eight people witnessed the stabbing death of Kitty Genovese and no one came to her aid or even bothered to call the police (White 2004, 155). Watching someone get murdered may not be illegal, but it is an iniquity.

Evil is often defined today as the absence of good. When God created light, he declared it to be good (Gen 1:3). The absence of light, darkness, could be thought of as evil—the absence of good without a pejorative inference.

Pejorative Evil

Viktor Frankl (2008) was a Jewish psychiatrist interned in the concentration camps by the Germans during the Second World War. His tips to prospective camp inmates on how to survive the camps offer insight into the nature of pejorative evil:

1. Don't draw attention to yourself from sadistic guards.[2]

2. Shave daily, walk briskly, and stand up straight to look healthy enough for work.

3. Applaud profusely when sadistic guards read poetry.

4. In walking in formation, stay in the middle or the front to avoid those that stumble and the beatings that follow.

5. Offer free psychiatric counseling to guards in need of it.

The key term in this description is sadistic. Evil pollutes those that touch it encouraging further evil—those abused often themselves become abusers.

This cycle of evil is not an urban legend. Stanfard (2008, 204) reports that:

> Approximately 70 percent of borderline personality disorder (BPD) patients report that they were sexuality abused as a child.

The male BPD patients are the classic wife beaters, while the female

BDP patients specialize in emotional abuse. As a consequence, spouses of BPD patients are at a high risk of suicide.

True evil is never simply the absence of good.

The Final Solution

Many people avoid making decisions hoping that they can escape accountability for their actions. Hannah Arendt was a student of Martin Heidegger and German Jew who, having escaped Nazi death camps before coming to America, was asked to cover the Adolf Eichmann trial in Jerusalem (1961) for the *New Yorker* magazine. Eichmann was the German officer who organized Adolf Hitler's program of extermination of the Jews known as the *Final Solution.*

Arendt attended the trial, expecting to see a hateful, anti-Semite, only to discover that Eichmann appeared as more of a petty bureaucrat. The face of evil at the Eichmann trial was that of someone unable or unwilling to think for themselves (Arendt 1992, 97–101).

Arendt's description of Eichmann cut me to the core. As I read her description, I worked in an office tasked with preventing financial calamities like the Great Recession, which nevertheless was unfolding in front of us. I could see many *little Eichmanns* inhabiting the offices as I passed down the hall. Blamires (2005,

27) observed: *"Eichmann is the archetype of our age, the supreme Organization Man. He kept the system going."*

The Eichmann trial changed Arendt forever. Afterwards, she devoted her life to studying the mind and coined the phrase *banality of evil,* which speaks to the commonplace nature of evil (Arendt 1976, 3). In some sense, denying the reality of evil is intellectually on par with denying the existence of the Holocaust.

Arendt's impressions of Eichmann have recently been revisited after the discovery of interviews that Eichmann gave before he was captured. Rosenthal (2011) writes:

> On leaving Berlin at the end of the war, Eichmann claims he told Muller, his superior: 'I will gladly jump into my grave in the knowledge that five million enemies of the Reich have already died like animals.' He is happy not only because the millions died – but because they died like animals.

These new insights should come as no surprise—human motivation is best pictured as an onion with many layers.

The Importance of Purpose

James K. A. Smith offers an interesting ethical insight into the nature of evil—an instrument (or person) is good when it is used with its purpose in view. When an instrument strays from its purpose, it commits sin and engages in evil.

Smith asks how one would evaluate a flute used to roast

marshmallows over a fire—we would never say that a flute used this way was a bad flute. Why? The measure of a flute is how it is used to play music, not how well it roasts marshmallows. Smith (2016, 89) observes:

> Virtue is bound up with a sense of excellence: a virtue is a disposition that inclines us to achieve the good for which we are made.

Because of original sin (e.g., Ps 51:5), we are not inclined to love virtues and to practice them. Being created in the image of God implies that we are on a mission in worship to develop the virtues through ritual and sacrament that match God's intent for our lives (Smith 2016, 88).

Satan in the Bible

Satan's role in tempting us and promoting evil in the world is found throughout scripture. In the Garden of Eden, Satan is pictured as a snake who rebels against God and tempts others to sin by rebelling with him.[3] God later advises Cain to be good because, otherwise, sin will strike like a snake crouching at your door (Gen 4:7).

Another important image of Satan is given in Job 1, where Satan is depicted as a ruthless prosecuting attorney in God's court. Satan's cruel lies slandered righteous Job. Still, Satan cannot afflict Job without first seeking God's permission (Job

1:6–12). In spite of Satan's cruelty, Job remains faithful. In the end, God not only acquits him of all of Satan's charges, Job is rewarded for his faithful perseverance (Job 42:10).[4]

In the synoptic gospels, the Holy Spirit leads Jesus into the desert where the devil tempts him.[5] Much like Adam and Eve are tempted with food, the devil starts by trying to goad a hungry Jesus to turn a stone into bread. The devil tempts Jesus three times. Jesus cites scripture in response to each temptation. In the final temptation, the Devil's temptation starts by misquoting scripture, but Jesus corrects the deception and resists the temptation.[6]

Unlike Adam, Jesus remains faithful to God's will in life and in death. Jesus' death on the cross then fulfills the prophecy of Satan's defeat (Gen 3:15) and pays the penalty for sin, so that we have been redeemed (Rom 5:12–14). Because the curse of sin is broken, the death penalty for sin has been rescinded (1 Cor 15:22). The resurrection, accordingly, proves that we have been reconciled with God.

In the Lord's Prayer, Jesus asks us to pray that we not be tempted and that we be delivered from evil. Because Satan must ask permission to tempt us, God can deny that petition and our deliverance is within his power. King David writes: *"Preserve me, O God, for in you I take refuge."* (Ps 16:1) Jesus has promised us that when we turn to him in weakness our salvation is secure (John 10:29).

A Place for Authoritative Prayer

> *In that hour he [Jesus] healed many people*
> *of diseases and plagues and evil spirits,*
> *and on many who were blind he bestowed sight.*
> *(Luke 7:21)*

Richard Foster (1992, 229) describes authoritative prayer with these words:

> In Authoritative Prayer, we are calling forth the will of the Father upon the earth. Here we are not so much speaking to God as speaking for God. We are not asking God to do something; rather, we are using the authority of God to command something done.

As practiced in the church today, authoritative prayer is also referred to as deliverance ministry, and, more popularly, as exorcism.[1] Foster's term, authoritative prayer, is more descriptive of the actual practice and less likely to evoke the baggage that accompanies other terms.

Background on Authoritative Prayer

Jesus practiced authoritative prayer, and even the most ardent critics of miracle healing admit that he did. One such critic, Sanders (1993, 149), for example writes:

> Exorcisms, which are a significant subcategory of healings, deserve fuller discussions. They were very important in Jesus' culture and also in his own career.

Sanders then proceeds to list twelve scriptural citations where Jesus performs exorcisms[2] and also lists exorcisms performed by others in the New Testament (Sanders 1993, 15). Significantly, Jesus also commissioned the disciples to preach and cast out demons (e.g., Mark 3:14–15).

The early church took the need to cast out demons seriously because virtually all adult converts had previously worshiped pagan idols, which were believed to be demons. The church commissioned exorcists much the same as we today ordain deacons and elders (Schmemann 1973, 69–71). The church has always recognized the need for authoritative prayer, even if some traditions have seldom openly practiced it.

Recent interest in authoritative prayer started with a Roman Catholic priest by the name of Francis MacNutt in the 1960s, who taught that authoritative prayer could be described as one of four types of healing needing prayer:

1. Repentance of sin (spiritual healing),

2. Emotional (or relational) healing,

3. Physical healing, and

4. Deliverance (healing from spiritual oppression) (MacNutt 2009, 130).

Distinguishing the different types of healing needs is important because many practitioners lump all healing needs into authoritative prayer and fail to distinguish spiritual oppression (common) from outright possession (rare).[3]

The Postmodern Need for Authoritative Prayer

The influence of rationalism in the modern period in Christian thought led many to question the reliability of scriptural references to miracles and especially exorcisms. This over-emphasis on rationalism seems increasingly out of place in the postmodern period when interest in the occult and magic has grown dramatically (Monetenegro 2006).

Why, if we believe in God, would we deny the existence of other spiritual beings that Jesus treated important enough to cast out?

About half the patients that I visited as a chaplain intern working in the emergency department at a local hospital were admitted for reasons that could be classified as preventable, such as problems arising out of poor lifestyle choices and other self-destructive behavior. In visiting later with the senior surgeon, he corrected my observation by reporting that the actual proportion of patients so classified was closer to three-quarters. Consequently, if in the concrete reality of medicine, we are incapable of maintaining our physical health in view of medical research, then how much more incapable are we of maintaining our own spiritual health?

More generally, United States is currently experiencing a thirty-year peak in suicides, with the largest increase among men between the ages of 45-and 64 (Tavernise 2016),[4] which has contributed to a three-year decline in life expectance in the United States (Bernstein 2018). If people are killing themselves in record numbers, spiritual oppression is likely part of the picture.

Outside of the medical and psychiatric fields, three factors suggest an increased need for authoritative prayer:

1. The growth of interest in pagan religions and immigration from countries where animistic religions are commonly practiced bringing to the West spiritual influences previously absent.

2. The mainstreaming of alternative sexual practices and drug use (and the abuse that often goes with them) has the potential to increase the number of individuals susceptible to spiritual oppression.

3. The discrimination of secular institutions practiced against Christians reduces the number of individuals who are nominally influenced by the church and thereby able to resist other spiritual influences.

This last observation is hotly debated among practitioners of deliverance ministry, with some saying that Christians can suffer spiritual oppression and others disagreeing. Implicit in this controversy is how one defines the Christian community.

For example, do cultural Christians suffer the same spiritual oppression as non-believers or not?

The Practice of Authoritative Prayer

A number of approaches have been taken in authoritative prayer, as described by sociologist Michael Cuneo (2001, xiv), who teaches at Fordham University (a Jesuit college in New York):

> American Exorcism is based on my personal interviews with exorcists and their clients, and my firsthand observation of more than fifty exorcisms...My primary concern is with exorcism as it's practiced among mainstream, predominantly middle-class Christians—the white-bread sector of American society...I am concerned simply with assessing the cultural significance of exorcism-related beliefs and practices in the contemporary United States, not with passing judgment on their ultimate validity.

Cuneo's storytelling, literature review, and personal interviews surpass anything that I have read about exorcism practices. The more typical author writing in this genre focuses on their own methods and experiences, which leaves the reader wondering whether the author's work is typical, reliable, and authoritative.

Cuneo (2001, 20) defines exorcism as follows:

> The rite of exorcism itself, according to [Malachi] Martin, is also a process consisting of several more or less distinct stages. At the outset the priest-exorcist is forced to contend with the pretense, a baffling (and sometimes protracted)

state in which the demonic present attempts to disguise its true identity and intentions. The breakdown occurs when the demon abandons subterfuge and begins to speak in its own voice; and during the next stage—what Martin refers to as the clash—the exorcist and demon become locked in a harrowing contest of wills for the soul of the possessed. Finally, if everything goes according to plan, the process concludes with the expulsion of the demonic presence.

Martin was a breakaway Jesuit Priest and the author of numerous books. The formal process of exorcism in the Catholic church is found in the Roman Ritual (Cuneo 2001, 259–260), which is a formal ceremony requiring the services of a priest and normally requires the approval of a bishop. Outside the Catholic church, exorcism can take a number of forms when performed by Pentecostals, Charismatics, and other Evangelicals, as Cuneo chronicles.

Cuneo's (2001, 275–277) concludes:

Some of the people who showed up for exorcisms seemed deeply troubled, some mildly troubled, and some hardly troubled at all. The symptoms they complained of—the addictions and compulsions, the violent mood swings, the blurred self-identities, the disturbing visions and somatic sensations—all of this seemed to me fully explainable in social, cultural, medical, and psychological terms...The same with the antics I sometimes witnessed while the exorcisms were actually taking place, the flailing and slithering, the shrieking and moaning, the grimacing and growling—none of this, insofar as I could tell, suggested the presence of demons.

He observes that exorcism may have a kind of placebo effect, suggesting that he remains a skeptic.

Concepts Supporting Authoritative Prayer

A couple of theological concepts inform this method, but are not necessarily required.

First, our souls are composed of our will, our mind, our memory, and our social environment. A modern word for soul might be our identity. The idea that our identity is socially held means that when we make Christ the cornerstone of our identity, we are not easily shaken the way that we might be if some other cornerstone were chosen. Treating Christ as a secondary part of our identity does not provide nearly the stability required to resist temptation and evil. As temptation and evil become more prevalent in the postmodern period, the need for this stability is greater than ever.

Second, the image of an evil spirit being confronted in authoritative prayer is that of a parasite. An evil spirit is parasitic in the sense that it cannot exist independent of its host for very long, much like a tick would starve in the absence of a new host. Driving it out therefore risks that the parasite will seek another local host and the prayer must account for this behavior.

Third, evil spirits are driven out, not by shouting, employing incantations, or any special form for prayer, but by denying that they have permission to inhabit the person being prayed over and appealing to the power and authority of God. Evil spirits act like bad lawyers, arguing for their rights to oppress a person. Thus, it is important to have the person's permission to pray because it implies that the demons do not have permission to continue their oppression.

Limits to Progress

*T*he idea of progress arose out of the technological euphoria of the modern era and entered theology in the nineteenth century with the euphoria over the abolition of black slave trading and ownership. However, the idea that progress is an inevitable or irreversible force remains economically and culturally tenuous.

While the specific reasons for economic and cultural reversals will always be unique, the general reason to be suspicious of economic and cultural progress is that progress is a cultural artifact that changes with circumstances.

If cultural progress is an historical anomaly, especially in view of the economic stagnation that many Americans face, what conditions support it?

Economic Progress

Standards of living rose in the United States after the Second World War for at least two reasons that no longer apply. First, the war destroyed many of our competitors worldwide, which led to strong international demand for U.S. goods and services. Second, local markets within the country were opened up to competition from outside firms and local cultures were eroded through universal education, consisting of both new knowledge and indoctrination in the national culture. This rationalization of different industries and regions have come to an end with the construction of the interstate highway system, national media, national banking, and the internet.

Once diminishing returns to new investment have been reached, the cost of implementing new ideas rises. From that point forward, additional growth can only come from demographic growth, technological innovation, or forcing others to pay our bills. Falling fertility rates and poor choices with respect to education and public expenditures suggests that we are not focused on making public policy choices consistent with growth.

Bacevich (2008, 31–36) sees this economic crisis dating back to public debts accumulated during the Vietnam War. Jimmy Carter spoke about this problem in his famous *Malaise Speech* (July 15, 1979) where he spelled out the need to live within our means if the American way of life were to be preserved. The American people rejected his analysis, and elected Ronald Reagan to the Presidency who began a policy of increasing public borrowing primarily to grow our military and of restructuring of the economy to enhance U.S. competitiveness in world markets. Decisions made in the Reagan years led to merger of banks and other firms into large corporations, set the stage for an increasingly interventionist U.S. foreign policy, and led to the abandonment of the American way of life that we have seen since the 1980s.

In this new environment of slower growth, social groups have had to compete for limited resources and opportunities. Outside of deliberate policies to focus economic resources on the most productive investments and to maintain equal opportunities for all groups, standards of living will decline for all but the favored groups able to maintain and expand their relative position. This competition makes it unlikely that everyone will share equally in economic progress.

Cultural Progress

The abolition of black slavery in the nineteenth century is a source of pride for many people. In my case, I am named for my great-great-grandfather, Stephen DeKock, who, as a young man, volunteered to fight for the Union in the American Civil War. Success in abolishing slavery motivated latter efforts to expand voting rights to women and minorities, to prohibit alcohol consumption, and to prohibit age, sex, and gender discrimination.

A byproduct of the Civil War seldom mentioned in this

context was the formation of large corporate firms that supplied Northern troops and developed weapons of mass destruction, such as iron clad ships, submarines, the Gatling gun, and repeating rifles. Modern warfare (war on civilians) is said to have begun with Sherman's *March to the Sea* in Georgia, which starved the Confederacy into submission. These innovations paved the way for the United States to become a super power (the American empire) over the decades that followed and, as a consequence, fueled the economic expansion that led to the economic and social progress that we enjoy as Americans.

The abolition of black slavery is unlikely to be reversed, but slavery itself has not so much gone away as it has been re-defined. Many former slaves in the rural South became share croppers, who were technically free, but caught in debt to their former masters. During much of the twentieth century, American men were involuntarily drafted into the military and forced to fight in foreign wars, including the First and Second World Wars and the wars in Korea and Vietnam. For women caught up in gangs, drugs, and prostitution, a different kind of slavery exists that has never really gone away.

While nasty institutions like slavery, debt-enslavement, and prostitution will probably continue to exist in the shadows of society, major reversals in the number of slaves occurred during the Second World War. Nazi Germany rounded up millions of Jews, political dissidents, and undesired groups, and placed them in concentration camps, where many were worked to death. Japan had similar policies. The U.S. had its own internment camps, but did not employ slave labor. Today such camps continue in communist countries, like North Korea.

The point of raising these examples is not to throw salt in old wounds, but to highlight the tenuous nature of human rights and notions like historical progress. If progress is a cultural artifact and can be reversed by changing circumstances, it is not inevitable or irreversible. The key question is: What foundation supports these rights and progress itself?

Cultural Reversal

The dominant cultural motif in the Bible is not progress, but proclivity of individuals and nations to sin. The most apt metaphor for progress is found in Genesis with the story of the Tower of Babel (Gen 11:1–9), but other metaphors can be found.

Although we are created in the image of God, original sin polluted both our hearts and minds by instilling a rebellious spirit in us. Human sin, after Adam and Eve left the Garden of Eden, grew to the point that God destroyed most of humanity with a flood (Gen 5:5). However, starting out fresh with a new family, Noah's, proved not to improve the faithfulness of humanity after the original sin of Adam and Eve (Gen 3:6). Even Jacob's sons, the fathers of the Nation of Israel, sinned in selling their brother, Joseph, as a slave to the Egyptians (Gen 37:28).

What should we conclude from the witness of Genesis? The idea that forming a community will somehow result in progress towards righteousness among fallen human beings is unfounded. The biblical expectation cited earlier is the Deuteronomic Cycle: doing evil, angering YHWH enough to produce historical subjugation, crying to the Lord in need, and raising up a deliverer (Deut 30; Brueggemann 2016, 59). This is not an endorsement of cultural progress, but rather of divine intervention in spite of human proclivity to sin.

From my earlier model of culture, reversal of progress is expected when any culture comes under stress and, as a dying culture, takes on the attributes of a traditional culture. Reversals normally occur on the outbreak of war or during economic crises. However, even in the absence of large-scale war and other stress, the large corporations that now dominate markets throughout the world frequently have traditional cultures that profoundly influence their employees from morning to night. Democratic rights, such as free speech, are routinely denied to corporate employees, and even legislatively mandated employee rights, such as unionization rights and whistler-blower protections, are scarcely available to employees unable to afford legal counsel. Consequently, the supposedly inevitable and irreversible cultural progress has not been obtained, and any progress that we have witnessed should be seen as a gift from God, not as an historical force or natural right.

Christian Foundations

The only glimmer of hope cited in the Bible is the death and resurrection of Jesus Christ that led to the giving of the Holy Spirit and the founding of the church (Acts 2:1–4). Yet, outside of faith, even the church is a fallen institution, as we read in the first three chapters of Revelation.

The warning in Revelation of special concern to the postmodern church is the letter to the church at Laodicea. John writes:

> I know your works: you are neither cold nor hot. Would that you were either cold or hot! So, because you are lukewarm, and neither hot nor cold, I will spit you out of my mouth. For you say, I am rich, I have prospered, and I need nothing, not realizing that you are wretched, pitiable, poor, blind, and naked. (Rev 3:15–17)

We could imagine the postmodern church sharing in tribulations similar to those articulated in Deuteronomic Cycle that applied earlier to the Nation of Israel. More generally, Revelation talks about a great tribulation (Rev 7:14) that will occur before the second coming of Christ. This tribulation has all the markings of a reversal of cultural progress and should serve as a reminder that our only hope is in Christ.

Does Faith Matter?

*T*he moment that we discover that faith in God under-girds all that we think, feel, or do, our attitude about faith changes. If faith is a logical necessity, then the quality of our faith becomes important. Are we going in all directions with an unreflective faith in a vague god of our own imagination or do we believe in God almighty, the maker of heaven and earth whose son, Jesus Christ, walked among us and died for our sins?

For the skeptic, the next question is: Does it really matter what we believe?

Conducive to Rationality

In studying epistemology in the previous chapters, I have implicitly argued that faith matters because it is conducive to rational thought and behavior. We worship God, who identifies with truth, as when God revealed himself to Moses:

> The LORD passed before him and proclaimed, The LORD, the LORD, a God merciful and gracious, slow to anger, and abounding in steadfast love and faithfulness, (Exod 34:6)

The word translated as faithfulness (תֶמֶא; amuth) in the Hebrew means both faithfulness and truth. The King James Bible translates this word as truth.

This focus on truth is conducive to rational inquiry, as is

obvious from many points of view. If truth was not important, Christianity might as well focus on mystery or fantasy, as many other religions do.

History of Public Education

Christians have always linked their faith to their actions. Jesus' brother James writes:

> But be doers of the word, and not hearers only, deceiving yourselves. For if anyone is a hearer of the word and not a doer, he is like a man who looks intently at his natural face in a mirror. For he looks at himself and goes away and at once forgets what he was like. (Jas 1:22–24)

Thus, we expect that Christians will act on their beliefs.

Because the Bible plays such a prominent role in Christian faith, Christians have always promoted literacy and education. The oldest universities in Europe were all started by the Catholic Church. Smith (2001, 96) reminds us:

> Universities evolved in Europe from cloisters; the word college initially referred to cloisters of monks who needed to know how to read in order to perform their offices.

Public education in Europe began with an academy begun by John Calvin and in America began as church Sunday school programs designed to help children learn to read their Bibles.

American Colleges

The oldest colleges in America also started out as Christian schools, even if they later wandered from their Christian roots. The reason for this was that before the twentieth century, about half of all university students aspired to become pastors, who were the best educated people in most towns and villages (Smith 2001, 79).

One such young man was David Brainard. Brainard got into trouble because of a private conversation:

> In 1742 he was expelled from Yale College when he claimed that one of his teachers did not have any more of God's grace than a wooden chair (Noll 2002, ix).

Local churches appealed Brainard's expulsion from Yale, but after Yale refused to re-admit him the churches went on to found Princeton University.

Because of his expulsion, Brainard could not be ordained, so he embarked on a career as a missionary to the Indians in New York, Pennsylvania, and New Jersey. Brainard later died of tuberculosis at the age of twenty-nine leaving behind his journals that were later edited and published by Jonathan Edwards (Noll 2002, ix–x). His journal inspired several generations of missionaries in the nineteenth century to evangelize the entire world.

For his part, Jonathan Edwards went on to inspire the Great Awakening and serve as Princeton's first president.

Brainard was not the only Christian to significantly influence American education. The first college in America to admit women and men together in 1834 was Oberlin College in Ohio, whose president at the time was evangelist Charles Finney, who played a key role in the Second Great Awakening. Oberlin became a model for other Christian colleges that campaigned for women's rights, abolition of slavery, and temperance (Dayton 2005, 35–43).

Benefits of Rationality

Our faith can also promote economic development. Two recent studies show that churches and missions can have a direct and long-term effect—the halo effect—on the communities that they serve.

First, Mike Wood Daly studied the spillover effects of congregations in Toronto, Ontario, Canada, following methods employed in an earlier study in Philadelphia, Pennsylvania. He writes:

> When applied in twelve congregations [10 Christian; 2 Islamic], the methodology revealed an accumulated 'halo effect' or economic

contribution of $51,850,178. The estimate translates into an average value of $4,320,848 per congregation. Even the smallest of the congregations studied, a Presbyterian Church with approximately 150 members and an annual operating budget of $260,000, was estimated to have an annual halo effect of $1.5 million. (Daly 2016, 9)

The study looked at seven spillover effects: open space, direct spending, education, magnet effect, individual impacts, community development, and social capital and care.

Second, economist Felipe Valencia Caicedo studied the residual impact of education provided by Jesuit priests in missions in Brazil that were later closed. He writes:

The Jesuit order founded religious missions in 1609 among the Guarani, in modern-day Argentina, Brazil and Paraguay. Before their expulsion in 1767, missionaries instructed indigenous inhabitants in reading, writing, and various crafts. Using archival records, as well as data at the individual and municipal level, I show that in areas of former Jesuit presence—within the Guarani area—educational attainment was higher and remains so (by 10%–15%) 250 years later. These educational differences have also translated into incomes that are 10% higher today. (Caicedoy 2018, Abstract)

While faith and education may not necessarily go together, this research brings to mind a passage in Exodus:

[The Lord] keeping steadfast love for thousands,

forgiving iniquity and transgression and sin, but who will by no means clear the guilty, visiting the iniquity of the fathers on the children and the children's children, to the third and the fourth generation. (Exod 34:7)[1]

Normally, people focus on the curse in the second part of this verse, but the first part is instructive in reading the Caicedo study. The Jesuit missions imparted a blessing still measurable two hundred and fifty years after they closed. While two hundred and fifty years is not a thousand generations, it is a blessing of twelve generations—roughly three times the length of time involved in the stated curse.

Answers to Prayer

The focus on rationality is seldom mentioned by Christians when they talk about why they came to faith, but everyone has a story about how God answers prayer and performs miracles.

In my own case, I could not have supported my family and gone to seminary, but for two rather arbitrary events—the dates of my joining and leaving federal employment. I joined the federal government two weeks (one pay period) before they abolished the old federal retirement system, something that meant nothing to me back in 1983. I left the government at year-end 2010, announcing my retirement a week before my division was abolished—on the exact same day as my departure date. If either of these dates had changed, I could not have earned as generous a pension, and seminary would have been financially out of reach.

Coincidence? Perhaps. But not everyone prays to a God who loves and cares for people because he created them in his own image. Human rights stem from our creation in God's image. Does it matter? It mattered to me.

Salvation and Eternal Life

*A*lot of people scoff at the idea that salvation and eternal life are real. Skepticism about the resurrection of Jesus Christ led the Apostle Paul, for example, to write: *"if Christ has not been raised, then our preaching is in vain and your faith is in vain."* (1 Cor 15:14) The resurrection of Christ implies that Jesus lives and will return someday to bring us home.

The Mechanics of Resurrection

Knowing that the future is in Christ, through faith we know that the future is secure and good, because we serve a God who loves us and is himself holy and good. Jesus reminds us:

> Everyone then who hears these words of mine and does them will be like a wise man who built his house on the rock. And the rain fell, and the floods came, and the winds blew and beat on that house, but it did not fall, because it had been founded on the rock. (Matt 7:24–25)

If Jesus is my rock, my denominator in life, and my assumption taken from outside the system, I cannot be easily shaken. But not everyone is convinced. How do we know the sequence of events in our salvation and the path to our eternal life?

The Apostle Paul outlines the path to salvation, saying:

> That I may know him and the power of his resurrection, and may share his sufferings, becoming like him in his death, that by any means

possible I may attain the resurrection from the dead. (Phil 3:10–11)

In other words, I know that I will be raised from the dead because I have known Christ, have shared in his suffering and death. While Christ accomplished our salvation by means of his life, death, and resurrection (Rom 5:6–11), we are sanctified in following Christ's model, the perfect of the image of God in human form.

Faith and the Soul

In his letter to the church in Corinth, Paul writes again on this subject:

> For just as the body is one and has many members, and all the members of the body, though many, are one body, so it is with Christ. For in one Spirit we were all baptized into one body—Jews or Greeks, slaves or free—and all were made to drink of one Spirit. For the body does not consist of one member but of many. (1 Cor 12:12–14)

Here Paul is talking specifically about the nature of the church, but a second interpretation is possible.

In Christian thinking, we often talk about the soul, which today we might refer to as our identity. In Hebrew thinking, the word *soul* implies body, mind, spirit, and the people who we are in relationship with. When we come to Christ, the Holy Spirit comes into our lives, the means by which we come into relationship with God. Our soul has forever changed. Much like we are one body in Christ (the church), we are also one with God, who is eternal.

Being one with God implies that our identity is now held in common with fellow believers past, present, and future. Because God is eternal, being in union with God implies that our identity is now eternal.

Example From Alzheimer's Disease

For those of you unaccustomed to this notion of shared identity and the soul, what happens to your identity when your mind is taken over with a disease, like Alzheimer's? Do you stop being a person? Do you lose your identity because you no longer remember who you are? Not at all. When you meet a person with Alzheimer's, their identity is retained by the people around them who care for them, order their favorite foods, and tell their stories.

It is no different when we die. When we die, our identity is retained not only by all of the people that knew us, but also, for the Christian, by the Holy Spirit, who is eternal. God who created us from dust can easily recreate us, complete with our identity, our souls, because we are in relationship (1 Cor 15:51–55).

POSTSCRIPT

Summary

*H*ere in the West, we inhabit a post-Christian society that challenges faith, but offers no viable alternative, strips life of meaning, and leaves us to sort out things for ourselves. Epistemology, the study of how we know what we know, provides a more systemic method for sorting things out.

Our need to have confidence that what we know is true because life is too short to test every assumption for ourselves. Imagine a world in which we argued about the definitions of red, yellow, and green every time we pulled up to a stoplight? In this ad hoc information age, it is important to examine basic assumptions in our thinking much like it is important to build a house on a solid foundation. Faith is not optional; neither is the epistemological task.

What we know is contingent on who we are as human beings. Confidence is not a mind-game; it also depends on our emotional response. The heart and mind are intimately connected. Our emotions reflect our assessment of threats to our being, social position, and livelihood. Who could concentrate on studying Einstein's theory of relatively if you thought the roof would cave in any moment? (Jung 1955, 112) Being part of a cause greater than ourselves provides security and meaning to life that cannot be obtained as individuals, a source of comfort that what we believe to be true is also in our best interests in view of our human vulnerability.

Uses and Abuses of Information

The scientific method hangs critically on the skill and intuition with which felt needs are transformed into problem definitions. The assumptions used in this intuitive process work essentially the same way as faith informs our daily life.

The language we speak shapes our perceptions of reality in fundamental ways, not the least of which is that it reflects the culture in which we live and worship. Our attitudes about gender, work, faith, and many other things are embedded in the words that we use and do not use. We are not alone in this world, even in our own thoughts and feelings—we carry our community with us wherever we go.

Learning Behavior

How we learn depends on proper mental function unencumbered by environmental stresses, disorders, disfunction, or pathologies, and directly affects the quality of decisions we make.

Under the best of circumstances, learning processes pose their own challenges. Behavioral learning processes can lead to logical traps, while rational learning processes can be infinitely postponed in the search for more information. In this context, the scientific method can help organize learning processes and improve problem solving. But, moral training and the use of mentors helps avoid logical traps, reducing search costs and increasing learning efficiency.

Decision-Making

Decisions and how we make them define an important part of who we are, separating the successful from the unsuccessful, the faithful from the unfaithful, and the men and women from the boys and girls. In an ideal world, we would approach important decisions employing proper mental function. That is, as well-informed adults devoid of dysfunctions, like mental illness or drug use, understand our own weaknesses, and considering carefully the options presented to us, taking our time to consult with our mentors, friends, and family (Plantinga 2000, 108–134).

In the corporate world, mistakes are inevitable. Learning the right lessons from mistakes requires a willingness to consider whether the decisions taken were flawed or merely untimely. The typical response of refusing to repeat an activity cuts short the process of assessment and discourages staff from taking responsibility for their role in it. Firing the manager responsible makes matters worse because the firm loses the manager best acquainted with what happened and because other staff will then be more reluctant to take risks in the future. Healthy organizations promote *"constructive dialogue"* about both project successes and failures (Stanton 2012, 10).

At a personal level, we need to go through this same deliberative process when problems arise. Confessing our sin and accepting God's forgiveness helps us take responsibility for our problems; accepting Christ as Lord and Savior means that we accept the Holy Spirit as a lifelong mentor (Acts 2:38). Starting on this process at a young age assures the greatest benefit from a life of faith.

Culture

I present a model of culture that pictures culture as the cumulative deviations from perfect rationality in making decisions. Christian culture is defined similarly as deviations (sin) from perfectly following the example of Christ. While this definition of culture may seem unduly negative, it allows us to understand the critical role of decisions and learning in our cultural development and to maintain a healthy skepticism of the role of culture in our lives.

Who is God?

In the above review of information, learning, and decision-making, what stands out is not how easy it is to believe in God, but how unlikely it is that we should encounter and come to faith. The Good News of the Bible is that God seeks us out and reveals himself to us in spite of numerous obstacles. Whether we respond in faith or not, we become like the gods that we choose to worship.

Being created in God's image implies that we should emulate God's ethical character. In his self-disclosure to Moses, God describes himself in terms of virtues—merciful, gracious, patient, loving, and faithful (Exod 34:6)—and relates to his people primarily through covenants and his written word.

Furthermore, God reveals himself in three persons: Father, Son, and Holy Spirit. We experience him both in his transcendence (God above) and immanence (God with us). In our own faithfulness, we emulate God as a model for our own lives. In our sin, we idolize other persons and things, and try to redefine God's covenantal love to serve our own needs.

Arguments About God's Existence

The Bible does not argue the existence of God because virtually everyone in the ancient world believed in gods of some sort. Intellectual arguments for God's existence in the postmodern era seldom provide sufficient evidence to compel belief because heart and mind are not equally engaged. Greek dualism, which stipulates that heart and mind are separate entities, pervades modern and postmodern thinking, and weakens apologetics based solely on the heart or the mind.

Where moderns concentrated on seeking objective truth, postmoderns prefer to ask who has the best story. When heart and mind are seen as inseparable, apologetics actually becomes easier. Things like hospitality become important in sharing the Good News. The proclivity of the Gospel's biggest critics to become believers—when they take time to understand it— underscores the resilience of the Gospel message.

Implications

Our identity is in Christ, the measure of everything else in our lives. When it is not, we commit the sin of idolatry and open ourselves up to greater sin because we have lost the image in which we were created.

The identity problem of individuals is written large in the church. The church, having been created by the Holy Spirit, is in a relational sense created in the image of the Trinity—an eternal, divinity community in perfect harmony. The authority of the church arises from divine revelation and the Bible.

Having strayed from scripture, the church has modeled

poorly formed spiritual boundaries marked by confessional wanderlust, an excessive focus on youth, balkanization of age groups, and minimization of sin. As evil has been minimized in church teaching and religious practice, it has grown unabated in society. The need has arisen to rethink the attitude about things like authoritative prayer and our future salvation in Christ.

The Better Story

How do we know what we know is true?

The end of the modern era spells the end of the modern pretension that we can logically prove that objective truth is knowable and provable. It is not. Because it is not knowable and provable in the abstract, proof requires that truth be knowable and provable to a human audience. An argument must both make sense and feel right in the context of the human condition. In the context of a confusing and dangerous world, who has the best story, one that you can bet your life on?

The Gospel Story

The Gospel story is the story of Jesus' birth, life, ministry, death, and resurrection. This story is the focus of the four Gospels—Matthew, Mark, Luke, and John—in the New Testament, and of faith statements, like the Apostle's Creed.

Christianity began in a graveyard with the resurrection. The resurrection could not have occurred without Jesus' crucifixion and death which was, in turn, associated with his life and ministry. Because Jesus' life and ministry was chronicled looking back from the resurrection, each sentence in the New Testament should be prefaced with these words: Jesus rose from the dead, therefore . . . Jesus' life, ministry, suffering, death, and resurrection are the Gospel story.

Christians, like Mary Magdalene, are the ones running from the cemetery to tell the rest of the world that Jesus lives (Matt 28:8).

After the Gospels themselves, the story of Jesus is the subject of many New Testament sermons by both Peter (Acts 2:14–41; 10:34–43) and Paul (Acts 13:16–41). And Jesus' story continues, through the lives of his apostles, through historical witness of the church, and through faithful Christian even today.

Context for the Gospel

In Genesis 11:1–9, we read the story of how men schemed to build a tower up to heaven to force God to come down and bless their city. The God who created heaven and earth (Gen 1:1) looked down on this effort and just laughed. These devious and obviously stupid men thought that they could manipulate a god who stood outside of time and space having created both. To prevent further foolishness, God confused them with different languages so that they would not be able to scheme together any further.

Because God transcends the material world and time itself, no physical or metaphysical tower can reach up to heaven. Towers, temples, religions, philosophies, and sciences are equally vain. God must come down to us; we cannot reach up to him. The story of God's efforts to reach down to us is recorded in scripture; he himself came down in the person of Jesus of Nazareth (Matt 1; Luke 1). God reversed the curse of Babel on the day of Pentecost with the giving of his Holy Spirit and the founding of the church (Acts 2), the oldest, continuous institution known to humanity.

But this story is not over; the church is not a museum of the past. Jesus points to the future and promises to reunite with his disciples: *"And if I go and prepare a place for you, I will come again and will take you to myself, that where I am you may be also."* (John 14:3) Because the future is in Christ and we worship a loving and all-powerful God, we know that our future is secure.

END NOTES

Front Matter

[1] Polanyi (1962, 3–5) argues somewhat differently:

> This would imply that, of two forms of knowledge, we should consider as more objective that which relies to a greater measure on theory [Copernican theory] rather than on more immediate sensory experience [Ptolemaic system].

[2] Bonhoeffer (1995, 17) begins his study of ethics with a most enigmatic statement:

> The knowledge of good and evil seems to be the aim of all ethical reflection. The first task of Christian ethics is to invalidate this knowledge.

If only God knows good and evil, then ethical knowledge shows separation from God. Thus, this knowledge is the source of human shame. Conscience is no help, being more a measure of the gap among people (Bonhoeffer 1995, 17–25).

[3] Compare, for example, (Prov 1:7; Isa 11:1; 2 Cor 4:6; Phil 1:9) with (1 Cor 8).

INTRODUCTION

Overview

[1] In this text, I view the modern period beginning with the American Revolution (1776), and the postmodern period beginning in 1960. The post-Christian period can best be dated

to the *Roe v. Wade*, 410 U.S. 113 (1973) decision by the United States Supreme Court that legalized abortion. By contrast, Veith (1994, 192) sees modernism taking hold of the mainline churches with the Scopes Trial in 1925.

Incentive to Examine Faith

[1] If Christendom can be dated to Constantine's Edict of Milan in 313, then the relationship between church and state has been accepted for more than a thousand years.

> If Caesar can get Christians there to swallow the *Ultimate Solution* [of Adolf Hitler] and Christians here [in America] to embrace the [use of the atomic] bomb, there is no limit to what we will not do for the modern world [and compromise our basic Christian values]. (Hauerwas and Willimon 2014, 17–27)

How We Learn

[1]

> In 1912, Dietrich's father [Karl] accepted an appointment to the chair of psychiatry and neurology in Berlin. This put him at the head of his field in Germany, a position he retained until his death in 1948. (Metaxas 2010, 13)

[2] This review is not intended to be comprehensive, but only representative of the primary ways we learn. For a biblical perspective on learning in an educational context, see: Beechick (1982).

[3] Milton Erickson was famous for his ability to reach particularly difficult psychiatric patients through hypnosis; yet, under hypnosis, when presumably he had more leverage to offer patients suggestion, he preferred to tell them stories of healing, which allowed him to step around the problem of patient resistance (Rosen 1982, 75).

[4] Citing Gadamer and Ricoeur, Vanhoozer (1998, 106) notes that: *"Meaning is the result of a two-way encounter between text and reader."* In this sense, the postmodern sees no stable meaning. Rather, Vanhoozer reports:*"The text is a network of signs and other texts, radically open and indeterminate."* (Vanhoozer 1998, 111) Meaning requires a context Because deconstructive literary criticism places no priority on particular contexts, anarchy rules (Vanhoozer 1998, 138). The idea of dismantling texts in playful interpretation gives no comfort when, having deconstructed the biblical text, nothing is offered to replace it—a kind of theft of meaning and security. Despair is substituted for purpose yet there is no accountability (Vanhoozer 1998, 182–185).

The Importance of Meta-narrative

[1] Hiebert (2008, 28) prefers the word, worldview, which he describes as both a model of reality and a model for action.

[2] Consider when Dorothy pulled back the curtain on the Wizard of Oz (1939) to find a white-haired, old man (https://en.wikipedia.org/wiki/The_Wizard_of_Oz_(1939_film).

[3] Hiebert (2008, 29) sees a worldview having five functions as:

　　1. *"Plausibility structures that provide answers to our*

ultimate questions."

2. [Gives] *"us emotional security"*

3. [Validates] *"our deepest cultural norms."*

4. *"Helps us integrate our culture."*

5. *"Monitors culture change."*

Challenges to Faith

[1] Ganssle (2009, 4) observes that the New Atheists do not bother to valid their hypotheses with a deliberate strategy of innuendo that he describes as a Nietzschean genealogy—a genealogy given not to prove that one's family includes royalty, but to discredit the family (Ganssle 2009, 136–137).

[2] In his class presentations, Johnson (1986, 15) added a felt need, citing the influence of Dewey (1997, 72).

[3] Detweiler (2003, 23) observes: Jesus was more than a carpenter; he was a techie. The Greek word, τέκτων (Mark 6:3 BNT), usually translated as carpenter probably better describes a builder. Think about it. Palestine has a lot of deserts and rocks; it has very few trees—the primary input in carpentry. Detweiler (2003, 24) observes that Jesus does not talk about carpentry; most of his stories are not even about agriculture. His stories are about winepresses, millstones, olive presses, tombstones, cisterns, and so on—the technologies of his era. He talked about the things that he knew best. Detweiler prefers the translation *artisan*.

[4] The *New York Times* recently reported that suicide is now at a 30-year high and the increase in suicide is greatest for men

between the ages of 45 and 64 (Tavernise 2016).

[5] The premise in inadequacy advertising is to infer a story of personal inadequacy and to resolve the inadequacy through the purchase of a product. Inadequacy marketing is pervasive in modern media and, yet, would not have a very wide appeal if consumers felt well-adjusted and self-confident (Sacks 2012, 89).

[6] According to the Center for Disease Control and Prevention (CDC 2017, 2018), in 2015, there were 1.1 million people in the United States infected with Acquired Immuno-Deficiency Syndrome (AIDS). Two-thirds of them were gay men. The average lifetime treatment cost in 2010 dollars was: $379,668. Consequently, we are talking about a drug market of roughly half a trillion dollars, one of the largest drug markets around. Roughly 675,000 people have died in the United States from AIDS (CDC 2016).

Why We Care About Epistemology

[1] Guinness (2003, 145) describes prevailing attitude in the 1960s when he was a philosophy student as ABC—anything but Christian.

[2] Most surprising, the largest increase arose among men between the ages of 45 and 64 (Tavernise 2016)

USES AND ABUSES OF INFORMATION

Foundations for Faith and Life

[1] An example can be seen in economics as applied to price

theory. The U.S. economy requires one
price be set outside the economy (in the world market) to assure stability. In the nineteenth century, that price was gold, and the system was called the gold standard. Every price in the U.S. economy could be expressed in terms of how much gold it was worth, as the dollar functions that way. Economists refer to this principle as the fixed-point theorem.

The Problem of Rumination

[1] Technology connects us, but it more often isolates us from one another. A *"Facebook friend,"* for example, is denied a vote if you get tired of them and remove them as a friend. Real friends give us immediate feedback and require explanations (Turkle 2011).

[2] This is a form of escalation in which psychiatric patients amplify rather than dissipate any tension in conversation. Even polite disagreement quickly evokes an increasingly hostile response.

[3] Stress addiction is a situation in which stress becomes the norm in our lives. Peace and quiet upset us because we are unaccustomed to it. Because we cannot relax, stress threatens not only our mental well-being, but also our physical health.

[4] Loneliness in the company others is the theme of a book by Sherry Turkle (2011). Nouwen (1975, 25) sees loneliness as related more to addiction than to rumination. Blackaby (2012, 47) talks about getting stuck in a particularly sad or particularly happy season of life.

[5] https://en.wikipedia.org/wiki/Infamy_Speech

[6] The yoke (Matt 11:28–30) Jesus uses to describe the work of a disciples was a leather collar worn by a work animal, such as a horse, to allow them to bear the burden of the work without injury. Disciples bear the yoke of discipleship; spectators do not. This implies that the blessings of Jesus are available exclusively to disciples. This is what James, Jesus' brother, means when he says: *"But be doers of the word, and not hearers only, deceiving yourselves."* (Jas 1:22)

Authenticity

[1] https://en.wikipedia.org/wiki/Archimedes.

[2] Statisticians frequently talk about the problem of inferring causality from correlations, but they seldom write about it because it undermines a lot of popular, but spurious statistical procedures. Greene (1997, 816) provide a review of the problem in discussing a statistical procedure called Granger casualty, a kind of statistical work around.

LEARNING BEHAVIOR

The World of Perception

[1] The use of childhood explorations has a long history in philosophy. Dewey (1997, vii, 157–169) wrote at length about childhood thought patterns and though of students as young scientists susceptible to bad influences of some teaching methods that could dampen their natural aptitude and curiosity.

Behavioral Learning

[1] Behavioral trap arguments pose an analytically sophisticated version of the slippery-slope argument, which argues that a small step in a particular direction will invite later calamity (Share-Landau 2018, 135–138).

[2] The honey trap is so pervasive that Cross and Guyer picture it on their book cover. Still, the presentation of an apple to Eve is another form of the honey trap (Cross and Guyer 1980, 1).

Rational Learning

[1] Bonhoeffer (1976, 17) focuses not on pride, but on knowledge as a measure of original sin and our distance from God, arguing that only God truly knows what is good and evil because of his infinite knowledge.

[2] Compare, for example, (Prov 1:7; Isa 11:1; 2 Cor 4:6; Phil 1:9) with (1 Cor 8).

[3] Skinner (1972, 17–19) questioned the autonomy of rational thinking, arguing that human responses are not free of their environments (not uncaused or free) and should not be held accountable for responding to bad environments. In other words, rational learning has its limits.

[4] In an agricultural setting, even young children can provide value to the family by assisting with chores, which may alter outcomes here. Among those who have never experienced rural

life and have an abbreviated decision horizon, having children is often viewed exclusively in terms of cost.

Analysis Versus Synthesis

[1]

> But what does it say? The word is near you, in your mouth and in your heart (that is, the word of faith that we proclaim); because, if you confess with your mouth that Jesus is Lord and believe in your heart that God raised him from the dead, you will be saved. For with the heart one believes and is justified, and with the mouth one confesses and is saved. (Rom 10:8–10)

[2] This is a brief statement of *Big Idea* preaching as articulated by Haddon Robinson (2001, 33–46).

[3] For example, search for theology on: https://www.ebsco.com. Alternatively, visit the Museum of the Bible (https://www.MuseumOfTheBible.org)

The Scientific Method and Objective Truth

[1] In class, unlike in his book, Johnson (1986, 15) add a felt need as the first step following Dewey (1997).

[2] The Germans were not the only ones running these experiments. However, more typically the non-German experiments used volunteers.

[3] Postmodern authors argue not only that truth is not only socially constructed, it is also biased, power plays (Smith 2001,

15). For example, Bourdieu and Wacquant (1992, 13) write:

> Social and mental structures fulfill[s] crucial political functions. Symbolic systems are not simply instruments of knowledge, they are also instruments of domination.

[4]   https://boards.straightdope.com/sdmb/showthread.php?t=758787

[5] In his study of the history of wealth and power in America, Phillips (2002, xii) writes:

> A political history of the American rich must inquire far beyond the predictable concentration of assets, inequality, and conspicuous consumption. It must also purse troubling and crippling side effects: high levels of political corruption, the arrogance of global economic power, the twisting of the U.S. tax code, and the voter belief in the captivity of government to private interests.

Given this history, it is reasonable to observe that temperance of religion and intellectual power has proven to be a passing phenomenon.

[6] In the context of a business environment, Patterson and others (2012, 116–119) consider three types of stories as counter-productive in corporate discussions: victim, villain, and helpless

stories. In each case, the advocates provide no aid in solving problems and refuse to accept responsibility for outcomes. Consequently, no progress takes place and nothing gets done.

Cultural Adaptation

[1] The name of a characters in a novel (DeFoe 1719).

[2] Discussion adapted from (Hiemstra 2009).

[3] Inertia is the physical property expressed in Sir Isaac Newton's first law of motion: a body at rest tends to stay at rest, and a body in motion tends to stay in motion. Inertia leads organizations to resist change and discount low-probability events.

DECISION MAKING

Proper Mental Function

[1] The Greek word for think, λογίζομαι, means: *"to give careful thought to a matter, think (about), consider, ponder, let one's mind dwell on."* (BDAG 4598, 2) The word also carries a mathematical connotation as with the word, reckon (BDAG 4598, 1).

[2] Thompson (2011, 107) characterizes the entire Letter to the Philippians as focused on developing the proper frame of mind (φρονέω e.g., Phil 1:7).

[3] Ganssle (2009, 1–2) views the New Atheists as Sam Harris,

Daniel Dennett, Richard Dawkins, and Christopher Hitchens. Their work shares three things in common: passion, belief not only in atheism but the danger of believing in God, and their status as public intellectuals speaking outside their fields of experience.

Suboptimal Decision Environment

[1] If self-indulgence and a sense of entitlement are hallmarks of this crisis of immaturity, Bacevich (2008, 9) offers a political analysis. He writes:

> Centered on consumption and individual autonomy, the exercise of freedom is contributing to the gradual erosion of our national power.

[2] Schaeffer (2005, 206) observes that following Aldous Huxley's writing, recreation drug use became an ideology in itself.

[3] By the time our children reach the age of 17, they have spent 63,000 hours exposed to media, 11,000 hours in school, 2,000 hours with their parents, and only 800 hours in church (Baer and Boone 2007, 88).

[4] The National Institute of Health (NIH 2018) reported that 19.1 percent of American reported having any anxiety during the period 2001–2003, with a lifetime incidence of 33.1 percent.

[5] Fry (2017) reports:

> As of 2016, 15% of 25-to-35 year-old Millennials were living in their parents' home. This is 5

percentage points higher than the share of Generation Xers who lived in their parents' home in 2000 when they were the same age (10%), and nearly double the share of the Silent Generation who lived at home in 1964 (8%). It doesn't appear that a lack of jobs is keeping Millennials at home.

Decisions and Media Manipulation

[1] In Hispanic films, people still routinely consult a priest and/ or visit a chapel to pray, but not in English-language films. The last example of a chapel visit in an English film that I remember was in *Home Alone* (1990) starring Macaulay Culkin, Joe Pesci, and Daniel Stern.

[2] Maslow pictured a pyramid of needs in which the foundational needs were physiological, followed by safety, love and belonging, self-esteem, and self-actualization at the top of the pyramid (Sacks 2012, 130).

Decisions under Uncertainty

[1] Johnson and Quance (1972) referred to this dilemma as the *"overproduction trap"* that arises when a fixed investment is no longer viable in the market, but the producer continues to produce and sell at a loss, trying to recoup the lost capital.

[2] Ironically, this expression is attributed to Heraclitus of Ephesus (535 – 475 BC) who actually said: πάντα χωρεῖ καὶ οὐδὲν μένει (everything changes and nothing stands still). https://en.wikiquote.org/wiki/Heraclitus.

Experience and Presuppositions

[1] A linguist study of words for snow in Inuit confirmed as many as a hundred words for snow (Robson 2013) .

[2] Paraphrasing Plato, Gaarder (1996, 84) writes:

> A particular horse *'flows,'* naturally. It might be old and lame, and in time it will die. But the *'form'* of the horse is eternal and immutable.

[3] The power of words is again emphasized in a biblical context when we see how serious blessings and curses are taken. For example, after Jacob is caught stealing his brother, Esau's, blessing from his father, Isaac refuses to take back the blessing—much like God created the heavens and the earth with spoken words, blessings—once conferred—cannot be retracted.

[4] Hauerwas and Willimon (2014) dates the end of Christendom to 1963, when the movie theater in his hometown was first allowed to open on Sunday.

[5] Jefferson called his Bible: *The Life and Morals of Jesus of Nazareth.* https://en.wikipedia.org/wiki/Jefferson_Bible. Also see: http://americanhistory.si.edu/jeffersonbible.

WHO IS GOD?

Origin of the Bible

[1] The technical description in the Bible was the first publication to appear in widespread circulation as a codex (bound book)

(Metzger and Ehrman 2005, 15). Stone (2010, 14) cites the existence of 5,500 partial or complete biblical manuscripts, making it the only document from the ancient world with more than a few dozen copies existent.

[2] Luther completed translating the entire Bible in 1534 (Bainton 1995, 255).

[3] Luther translated the Apocrpha in 1534, but specifically said they were not canonical, just good to read (see: http://www.lstc.edu/gruber/luthers_bible/1534.php).

Interpreting the Bible

[1] Cardinal (later Pope) Ratzinger (1994, 33–34) writes:

> It is the task of exegetes to work…toward a better understanding and explanation of the meaning of Sacred Scripture in order that their research may help the Church to form a firmer judgment. For, of course, all that has been said about the manner of interpreting Scripture is ultimately subject to the judgment of the Church which exercises the divinely conferred commission and ministry of watching over and interpreting the Word of God.

[2] A few words in the New Testament and a small portion of the Old Testament are also written in Aramaic, the common language in first century Palestine.

[3] (e.g., Ps 86:15, Ps 103:8, Jonah 4:2).

Interpreting the Bible 2.0

[1] https://en.wikipedia.org/wiki/Adam_and_Steve.

[2] Fortson and Grams (2016, 251–258) discuss this issue of intent in Leviticus, as interpreted in the New Testament at great length.

God's Attributes in Creation

[1] Tozer (2014, 87) captures both the physical and metaphorical concepts when he writes:

> When we speak of God as transcendent, we mean of course that He is exalted far above the created universe, so far above that human thought cannot imagine it.

[2] Heaven and earth can also be interpreted as proxies for God's attributes of transcendence and immanence (Jer 23:23–24; Dyck 2014, 99).

[3] God's eternal nature is also defined with a merism: *"I am the Alpha and the Omega,"* says the Lord God, *"who is and who was and who is to come, the Almighty."* (Rev 1:8)

[4] This bird (avian) image appears again in the baptismal accounts of Jesus. For example, in Matthew 3:16, we read:

> And when Jesus was baptized, immediately he

went up from the water, and behold, the heavens were opened to him, and he saw the Spirit of God descending like a dove and coming to rest on him.

Image Theology

[1] Hoekema (1986, 1) turns the discussion of image around. Instead of asking who is God? He asks: Who are we?

God's Immutability

[1] God also shares his meekness with Moses (Num 12:3), and is prophesied in Zechariah 9:9 to be meek.

Context for God's Love

[1] Hafemann (2007, 33) writes:

> For as we have seen in the covenant formula, mutual belonging and 'love', like that between members of a family, becomes the 'glue' holding the covenant relationship between God and his people together,

[2] Hafemann (2007, 49–65) sees the new covenant articulated in Jeremiah 31:31–34, and best articulated in the New Testament in 2 Peter 1:3–11.

A God Who Listens

[1] Bonhoeffer (1976, 102) observed of atheism that:

> It is not the theoretical denial of the existence of

a God. It is itself a religion, a religion of hostility to God.

[2] McGrath (2004, 262) writes:

> If God is dead, Nietzsche pointed out, people would transfer their old faith in God to something else. They had to believe in something. With precocious foresight, Nietzsche declared that, having lost faith in God people would now put their trust in barbaric *'brotherhoods with the aim of robbery and exploitation of the non-brothers.'* For many, this was an alarming prediction— precisely because it was predictable—of the rise of the tribalism of the Nazis and other dubious groups.

[3] Schaeffer (2005, 180) observes:

> I am convinced that when Nietzsche came to Switzerland and went insane, it was not because of general disease, though he did have this disease. Rather it was because he understood that insanity was the only philosophical answer if the infinite-personal God does not exist.

Image Theology and Idolatry

[1] May (1988, 14–16) defines addiction as: *"A state of compulsion, obsession, or preoccupation that enslaves a person's will and desire"* and specifically relates it to idolatry.

ARGUMENTS ABOUT GOD'S EXISTENCE

Hebrew Anthropology and Apologetics

[1] In the story, church is where eight-year old Kevin McCallister meets Old Man Marley and finds out that he is not scary, but a nice man. The two become friends and help each other resolve their problems. ps://en.wikipedia.org/wiki/Home_Alone.

The Surprising Role of Storytelling

[1] Polanyi (1962, 4) writes:

> The new Copernican system was as anthropocentric as the Ptolemaic view, the difference being merely that it preferred to satisfy a different human affection.

That being a preference for theory over empirical observation.

Resilience of the Gospel

[1] The Koran refers to Jesus many times as a prophet, and even has a chapter on his mother, Mary.

Pascal's Wager

[1] Richard Swinburne's (1979) probabilistic argument for the existence of God builds on a similar argument. Clark (2001, 38) summarizes:

> 1. The existence and design of the world—including morality, free moral agents, religious experience—are

extremely improbable without the hypothesis of theism.

2. The hypothesis of theism significantly raises the probability of the existence of intelligent design of the world.

3. The hypothesis of theism explains and unites under a single hypothesis an otherwise disparate and unlikely set of phenomena—the existence of the world, religious experience, miracles, and evil.

4. The hypothesis of theism has sufficient intrinsic plausibility.

5. Therefore, it is likely that God exists.

[2] Smith (2001, 44) reported the original findings in this study as 28 percent, which substantially underestimated the final number of 46 percent.

[3] Also see: (Caicedoy 2018) and (Daly 2016).

Arguments for God's Existence

[1] Clark (2001, 97) rejects the evidentialist position and sees *"belief in God more like the belief that [other] persons have minds."* In other words, belief in God is much like receiving a phone call, talking with someone, and recognizing that they both exist and are a person, not a machine.

[2] Kreeft (1993, 56–58) summarizes a total of twenty-four arguments from philosophy for the existence of God.

[3] Clark (2001, 18) explains:

> There are two ways that statements can be true. Statements may be contingently true, which means that their being depends on something else; and statements may be necessarily true, which means that their truth is not dependent on the truth of any other statement.

Citing Richard Taylor, Clark (2001, 21) finds no reason to doubt that the universe's existence is contingent on something external that is imperishable, that is, God.

[4]   https://www.merriam-webster.com/dictionary/big%20 bang%20theory.

[5] Usually the argument about precision is couched in terms of constants from physics, not historical events (e.g., Smith 2001, 176–177).

[6] Ganssler (2009, 116–117) argues that Darwin's theory can be applied outside biology provided two conditions are met. First, one needs to demonstrate a benefit. Natural selection assists a species to survive better than competing species. Second, one needs to show a transmission method. Genes record favorable variations.

Arguments About Creation

[1] Building on the concept of a master race, Hitler tried also to reform the church in this image to turn Christianity from being, as Nietzsche described it—a slave religion into a *"master religion of the Nordic race"* (Meinecke 1969, 82).

[2] Smith (2001, 166) writes:

> Whether the Soviet death toll was one hundred million of its own people (which is probable) or a *'mere'* ten million (which is implausible), the eighty years of terror is unforgivable.

IMPLICATIONS

God is my Denominator

[1] Course entitled: *"Introduction to Church Music,"* Southwestern Baptist Theological Seminary, 1983 (Gigilio 2003, 140).

The Pathological Culture

[1] Smith (2001, 90) writes:

> The hermeneutics of suspicion is an interpretative device that attacks theses not heard-on. but indirectly by innuendo.

[2] (Tavernise 2016); Bernstein 2018).

The Church as an Authority

[1] https://www.rca.org (as of 16 November 2018).

[2] https://www.pcusa.org (as of 16 November 2018).

[3] Note the original language of the *Scot Confession*:
302—*Simple Faith*

The notes of the true Kirk, therefore, we believe, confess, and avow to be: first, the true preaching of the Word of God, in which God has revealed himself to us, as the writings of the prophets and apostles declare; secondly, the right administration of the sacraments of Christ Jesus, with which must be associated the Word and promise of God to seal and confirm them in our hearts; and lastly, ecclesiastical discipline uprightly ministered, as God's Word prescribes, whereby vice is repressed and virtue nourished. (PCUSA 1999, 3.18)

[4] Longfield (1991, 79–91) chronicles changes 1925–1936 in the Presbyterian Church from dropping the five fundamentals of faith as ordination requirements in 1925 to changes at Princeton Theological Seminary allow theological diversity within the denomination. These changes also effectively removed doctrinal basis for church discipline, except in the case of gross error.

The Myth of Perpetual Youth

[1] Bonhoeffer (1997, 105–107) anticipated this problem calling it the peril of the void and relating it to the coming last days. He writes:

With the loss of past and future, life fluctuates between the most bestial enjoyment of the moment and an adventurous game of chance. An abrupt end is put to any kind of inner self-development and to any gradual attainment of personal or vocational maturity. There is no personal destiny, and consequently there is no personal dignity.

Of course, he was writing from Nazi Germany, which some have referred to as the first postmodern society.

[2] Bonhoeffer (1997, 114) observes:

> The Church confesses herself guilty of the collapse of parental authority. She offered no resistance to contempt for age and idolization of youth, for she was afraid of losing youth and with it the future.

[3] Sacks (2012, 130) lists Abraham Maslow's needs as physiological (base), safety, love and belonging, self-esteem, to self-actualization.

[4] This is a theme of a popular song by U2: *"Stuck In A Moment You Can't Get Out Of"* (https://www.youtube.com/watch?v=emFUtuotHL4).

The Banality of Evil

[1] The reason why the church should ignore homosexual prohibitions in the Bible, Rogers (2009, 33) argued is that the church historically used the Bible to oppress blacks and women, and now it is using the Bible to oppress homosexuals. As former moderator of the General Assembly, Rogers succeeded in convincing the Presbyterian Church USA to reverse its ban on ordination of homosexuals and to allow gay marriage.

[2] Frankl (2008, 92) writes:

> When the SS took a dislike to a person, there was always some special man in their ranks known to have a passion for, and to be highly specialized in, sadistic torture, to whom the unfortunate prisoner was sent.

[3] For example, Kline (2006, 302) writes about the people of God and the people of the serpent.

[4] Along these same lines, Jesus said:

> Simon, Simon, behold, Satan demanded to have you, that he might sift you like wheat, but I have prayed for you that your faith may not fail. And when you have turned again, strengthen your brothers. (Luke 22:31–32)

[5] Mark 1:12–13 gives a brief overview, while Matt 4:1–11 and Luke 4:1–13 are longer. The Luke version has the most detail. The second and third questions posed by Satan appear in different order in Matthew and Luke.

[6] Each temptation Jesus faces is a challenge facing all Christians, particularly leaders. Nouwen (2002, 7–8) summarizes these leadership challenges as the temptation to be relevant (provide food), to be spectacular (show your divinity), and to be powerful (take charge).

A Place for Authoritative Prayer

[1] In the Catholic faith, exorcism is practiced primarily after other explanations for observed behavior have proven inadequate. Cuneo (2001, 12) writes:

> The rite of exorcism, in fact, is the only Catholic rite in which the officiating priest is advised to take an initial stance of incredulity. Rather than assuming possession straightway and proceeding

with an exorcism, the priest is supposed to rule out all other possibilities—from organic disorder to psychological pathology to outright fraud.

[2] Mark 1:23–8/Luke 4:31–37, Mark 1:32–34/Matt 8:16/Luke 4:41, Mark 1:19, Mark 3:11/Luke 6:18, Mark 3:20–30/Matt 12:22–37/ Luke 11:14–23, Mark 5:1–20/Matt 8:28–34/Luke 8:26–39, Mark 7:24–30/Matt 15:21–28, Mark 9:25/Matt 17:18/Luke 9:42, Matt 4:24, Matt 9:32–34, Luke 8:2, and Luke 8:2 (Sanders 1993, 149–150).

[3] MacNutt (2009, 167) distinguishes deliverance ministry (relief from spiritual oppression) from exorcism (relief from possession).

[4] I personally know of two men in that demographic who committed suicide in 2016.

Permanence

[1]   https://simple.m.wikipedia.org/wiki/Second_law_of_ thermodynamics.

Does Faith Matter?

[1] Also see Exodus 20:4–6 cited earlier.

REFERENCES

Adams, James Truslow. 1941. *The Epic of America*. Blue Ribbon Books.

Alchian, Armen. 1950. "*Uncertainty, Evolution, and Economic Theory.*" pp 211-221 of Journal of Political Economy. Vol 58.

Arendt, Hannah. 1992. *Lectures on Kant's Political Philosophy*. Chicago: University of Chicago Press.

Arendt, Hannah. 1996. *The Life of the Mind: The Groundbreaking Investigation of How We Think*. New York: Harvest Book.

Bacevich, Andrew J. 2008. *The Limits of Power: The End of American Exceptionalism*. New York: Metropolitan Books.

Baehr, Ted and Pat Boone. 2007. *The Culture-Wise Family: Upholding Christine Values in a Mass Media World*. Ventura: Regal.

BDAG. Greek-English Lexicon of the New Testament and Other Early Christian Literature. *2000*. The University of Chicago Press (electronic edition). Revised and edited by Frederick William Danker based on the Walter Bauer's Griechisch-deutsches Wörterbuch zu den Schriften des Neuen Testaments und für frühchristlichen Literatur, sixth edition, ed. Kurt Aland and Barbara Aland, with Viktor Reichmann and on previous English Editions by W.F.Arndt, F.W.Gingrich, and F.W.Danker.

Becker, Gary S. 1957. *The Economics of Discrimination*. Chicago: University of Chicago Press.

Beechick, Ruth. 1982. *A Biblical Psychology of Learning*. Denver: Accent Books.

Bernstein, Lenny. 2018. "U.S. life expectancy declines again, a dismal trend not seen since World War I." Washington Post. November 29.

Bettelheim, Bruno. 1976. *The Uses of Enchantment: The Meaning and Importance of Fairy Tales*. New York: Knopf.

Blackaby, Richard. 2012. *The Seasons of God: How the Shifting Patterns of Your Life Reveal His Purposes for You*. Colorado Springs: Multnomah Books.

Blamires, Harry. 2005. *The Christian Mind: Hoe Should a Christian Think? (Orig Pub 1963) Vancouver: Regent College Publishing*.

Blenkinsopp, Joseph. 1992. *The Pentateuch: An Introduction to the First Five Books of the Bible*. New York: Doubleday.

Bonhoeffer, Dietrich. 1976. *Ethics (Orig Pub 1955) Edited by Eberhard Bethge*. Translated by Neville Horton Smith. New York: MacMillan Publishers Company, Inc.

Bonhoeffer, Dietrich. 1995. *The Cost of Discipleship (Orig Pub 1937)*. New York: Simon and Schuster.

Bourdieu, Pierre and Loïc J. D. Wacquant. 1992. *An Invitation to Reflective Sociology*. Chicago: University of Chicago Press.

Bridges, William. 2003. *Managing Transitions: Making the Most of Change*. Cambridge, MA: Da Capo Press.

Brueggemann, Walter. 2016. *Money and Possessions*. Interpretation series. Louisville: Westminster John Knox Press.

Butterfield, Rosaria Champagne. 2012. *The Secret Thoughts of an Unlikely Convert: An English Professor's Journey into Christian Faith*. Pittsburgh: Crown & Covenant Publications.

Caicedoy, Felipe Valencia. 2018. *"The Mission: Human Capital Transmission, Economic Persistence, and Culture in South America."* Quarterly Journal of Economics. October. Online: https://doi.org/10.1093/qje/qjy024. Accessed: 4 January 2019.

Card, Michael. 2005. *A Sacred Sorrow: Reaching Out to God in the Lost Language of Lament*. Colorado Springs: NavPress.

Center for Disease Control (CDC). 2016. *"Today's HIV/AIDS Epidemic."* CDC Factsheet. Online: https://www.cdc.gov/nchhstp/newsroom/docs/factsheets/todaysepidemic-508.pdf. Accessed: 8 January 2019.

Center for Disease Control (CDC). 2017. *HIV Cost-effectiveness.* Online: https://www.cdc.gov/hiv/programresources/ guidance/costeffectiveness/index.html. Accessed: 8 January 2019.

Center for Disease Control (CDC). 2018. *Basic Statistics [on AIDS].* Online: https://www.cdc.gov/hiv/basics/statistics. html. Accessed: 8 January 2019.

Chan, Simon. 1998. *Spiritual Theology: A Systemic Study of the Christian Life.* Downers Grove, IL: IVP Academic.

Chandler, Jr. Alfred D. *2002.* The Visible Hand: The Managerial Revolution in American Business (Orig Pub 1977). Cambridge: Belknap Press.

Clark, Kelly James. 2001. *Return to Reason: A Critique of Enlightenment Evidentialism and ad Defense of Reason and Belief in God.* Grand Rapids: Eerdmanns.

Clinebell Jr, Howard J. 1978. *Understanding and Counseling the Alcoholic Through Religion and Psychology (Orig Pub 1956) Nashville: Abingdon.*

Cloud, Henry. 2008. *The One-Life Solution: Reclaiming Your Personal Life While Achieving Greater Professional Success.* New York: HarperCollins.

Crisk, Francis. 1994. *The Astonishing Hypothesis: The Scientific Search for the Soul*. New York: Simon and Schuster.

Cross, John G. and Melvin J. *Guyer*. 1980. Social Traps. Ann Arbor: University of Michigan Press.

Cuneo, Michael W. 2001. *American Exorcism: Expelling Demons in the Land of Plenty*. New York: DoubleDay.

Currie, David A. 2018. *"Shaped by the Word: Sola Scriptura for Spiritual Formation."* Pp 50-57 in Reformation Celebration: The Significance of Scripture, Grace, Father, and Christ. Gordon L. Isaac and Eckhard J. Schnabel ed. Peabody: Hendrickson.

Daly, Mike Wood. 2016. *Valuing Toronto's Faith Congregations*. June. Online: https://www.haloproject.ca/phase-1-toronto. Accessed: 3 January 2019.

Davies, Brian and G.R. *Evans [ed}*. 2008. Anselm of Canterbury: The Major Works. Oxford World Classics. New York: Oxford University Press.

Dayton, Donald W. 2005. *Discovering an Evangelical Heritage (Orig Pub 1976)*. Peabody: Hendrickson Publishers.

Defoe, Daniel. 1719. *The Life and Strange Surprising Adventures of Robinson Crusoe*. United Kingdom: William Taylor.

Desilver, Drew. 2018. *"For most U.S. workers, real wages have barely budged in decades."* Pew Research. August 7. Online: http://www.pewresearch.org/fact-tank/2018/08/07/for-most-us-workers-real-wages-have-barely-budged-for-decades. Accessed: 4 December 2018.

Detweiler, Craig. 2013. *iGods: How Technology Shapes Our Spiritual and Social Lives.* Grand Rapids: Brazos Press.

Dewey, John. 1997. *How We Think (Orig Pub 1910).* Mineola, NY: Dover Publications.

Duke University. 1999. *"Religious Attendance Linked to Lower Mortality in Elderly."* Updated: January 20, 2016. Online: https://corporate.dukehealth.org/news-listing/religious-attendance-linked-lower-mortality-elderly Accessed: 18 January 2019.

Dyck, Drew Nathan. 2014. *Yawning at Tigers: You Can't Tame God, So Stop Trying.* Nashville: Thomas Nelson.

Dyrness, William A. 2001. *Visual Faith: Art, Theology, and Worship in Dialogue.* Grand Rapids: Baker Academic.

Edwards, Jonathan. 2009. *The Religious Affections (Orig Pub 1746).* Vancouver: Eremitical Press.

Elliott, Matthew A. 2006. *Faithful Feelings: Rethinking Emotion in the New Testament*. Grand Rapids: Kregel Academic and Professional.

Evans, Craig A. 2005. *Ancient Texts for New Testament Studies: A Guide to Background Literature*. Peabody, MA: Hendrickson.

Ferry, Luc. 2011. *A Brief History of Thought: A Philosophical Guide to Living*. Translation by Theo Cuffe. New York: Harper Perennial.

Foley, Michael P. [editor] 2006. *Augustine Confessions (Orig Pub 397 AD)*. 2nd Edition. Translated by F. J. Sheed (1942). Indianapolis: Hackett Publishing Company, Inc.

Fortson, S. Donald and Rollin G. *Grams*. 2016. Unchanging Witness: The Consistent Christian Teaching on Homosexuality in Scripture and Tradition. Nashville: B&H Academic.

Foster, Richard J. 1992. *Prayer: Find the Heart's True Home*. New York: HaperOne.

Frankl, Viktor E. 2008. *Man's Search for Meaning: A Classic Tribute to Hope from the Holocaust (Orig Pub 1946)*. Translated by Ilse Lasch. London: Rider.

Fry, Richard. 2017. *It's Becoming More Common for Young Adults to Live at Home and for Longer Stretches*. Pew Research Center. May 5. Online: http://www.pewresearch.org/fact-tank/2017/05/05/its-becoming-more-common-for-young-adults-to-live-at-home-and-for-longer-stretches. Accessed: 26 November 2018.

Freud, Sigmund. 1961. *The Future of an Illusion (Orig Pub 1927)*. Edited and translated by James Strachey. New York: W.W. Norton and Company.

Friedman, Edwin H. 1985. *Generation to Generation: Family Process in Church and Synagogue*. New York: Guilford Press.

Gaarder, Jostein. 1996. *Sophie's World: A Novel About the History of Philosophy*. Translated by Paulette Møller. New York: Berkley Books.

Gagnon, Robert A. J. *2001. The Bible and Homosexual Practice: Texts and Hermeneutics*. Nashville: Abingdon Press.

Ganssle, Gregory E. 2009. *A Reasonable God: Engaging the New Face of Atheism*. Waco: Baylor University Press.

Geisler, Norman L. and Patrick Zukeran. 2009. *The Apologetics of Jesus: A Caring Approach to Dealing with Doubters*. Grand Rapids: Baker Books.

Giglio, Louis. 2003. *The Air I Breathe*. Colorado Springs: Multnomah Publishers.

Gilbert, Roberta M. 2006. *The Eight Concepts of Bowen Theory: A New Way of Thinking about the Individual and the Group*. Front Royal (VA): Leading Systems Press.

Gödel, Kurt. 1931. *Über formal unentscheidbare Sätze der Principia Mathematica und verwandter Systeme I ("On Formally Undecidable Propositions of Principia Mathematica and Related Systems I")*. pages 173-198 in Monatshefte für Mathematik und Physik. 38:1.

Greene, William H. 1997. *Econometric Analysis*. New Jersey: Prentice Hall.

Griswold, A. Whitney. *1934*. "Three Puritans on Prosperity," pp. 475-493 of New England Quarterly, Vol. VII, September.

Guinness, Os. 2003. *The Call: Finding and Fulfilling the Central Purpose of Your Life*. Nashville: Thomas Nelson.

Hafemann, Scott J. 2007. *"The Covenant Relationship."* pp 20-65 of Central Themes in Biblical Theology: Mapping Unity in Diversity. Edited by Scott J. Hafemann and Paul R. House. Grand Rapids: Baker Academic.

Hahn, Scott W. 2009. *Kinship by Covenant: A Canonical Approach to the Fulfillment of God's Saving Promises*. New Haven: Yale University Press.

Hart, David Bentley. 2009. *Atheist Delusions: The Christian Revolution and Its Fashionable Enemies*. New Haven: Yale University Press.

Hauerwas, Stanley and William H. Willimon. *2014*. Resident Aliens: A Provocative Christian Assessment of Culture and Ministry for People Who Know that Something is Wrong. Nashville: Abingdon Press.

Heifetz, Ronald A. and Marty Linsky. *2002. Leadership on the Line: Staying Alive through the Dangers of Leading*. Boston: Harvard Business School Press.

Hellerman, Joseph H. 2001. *The Ancient Church as Family*. Minneapolis: Fortress Press.

Hendricks, Scotty. 2018. *"God Is Dead: What Nietzsche Really Meant."* Online: http://bigthink.com/scotty-hendricks/ what-nietzsche-really-meant-by-god-is-dead. Accessed: June 8.

Hiemstra, Stephen W. 2009. *"Can Bad Culture Kill a Firm?" pp 51-54 of Risk Management*. Society of Actuaries. Issue 16. June.

Hoekema, Anthony A. 1994. *Created in God's Image*. Grand Rapids: Eerdmans.

HOLL - A Concise Hebrew and Aramaic Lexicon of the Old Testament. 1997. *Based upon the Lexical Work of Ludwig Koehler and Walter Baumgartner, edited by W.L.* Holladay. Brill Academic Publishers.

Hunter, George G. III. 2000. *The Celtic Way of Evangelism: How Christianity Can Reach the West...Again*. Nashville: Abingdon Press.

Johnson, Andrew. 2017. *If I Give My Soul: Faith Behind Bars in Rio de Janeiro*. New York: Oxford.

Johnson, Glenn L. 1986. *Research Methodology for Economists: Philosophy and Practice*. New York: MacMillan Publishing Company.

Johnson, Glenn L. and C. *Leroy Quance [editors]*. 1972. The Overproduction Trap in U.S. Agriculture: A Study of Resource Allocation from World War I to the Late 1960's. Baltimore: Johns Hopkins University Press.

Jung, Carl G. 1955. *Modern Man in Search of a Soul (Orig Pub 1933)*. Translated by W.S. Dell and Cary F. Baynes. New York: Harcourt, Inc.

Kaufman, Alexander C. 2017. *"Here Are The 379 Companies Urging The Supreme Court To Support Same-Sex Marriage."* (Orig Pub 2015) HuffPost. 6 December. Online: https:// www.huffingtonpost.com/2015/03/05/marriage-equality-amicus_n_6808260.html. Accessed: 8 January 2019.

Keller, Timothy. 2016. *Making Sense of God: An Invitation to the Skeptical*. New York: Viking Press.

Kinnaman, David and Gabe Lyons. 2016. *Good Faith: Being a Christian When Society Thinks You're Irrelevant and Extreme*. Grand Rapids: BakerBooks.

Kline, Meredith G. 2006. *Kingdom Prologue: Genesis Foundations for a Covenantal Worldview*. Eugene: Wipf & Stock Publishers.

Kreeft, Peter. 1993. *A Shorter Summa: The Essential Philosophical Passages of St.* Thomas Aquinas' Summa Theologia. Edited and Explained. San Francisco: Ignatius Press.

Kreeft, Peter. 2007. *The Philosophy of Jesus*. South Bend, IN: Saint Augustine Press.

Kuhn, Thomas S. 1996. *The Structure of Scientific Revolutions (Orig Pub 1962)*. Chicago: University of Chicago Press.

Lewis, C.S. 1955. *Surprised by Joy: The Shape of My Early Life*. New York: Harcourt Book.

Lewis, C. S. 2001. *Mere Christianity* (Orig Pub 1950). New York: Harper Collins Publishers, Inc.

Longfield, Bradley J. 2013. *Presbyterians and American Culture: A History*. Louisville: Westminster John Knox Press.

Longfield, Bradley J. 1991. *The Presbyterian Controversy: Fundamentalists, Modernists, and Moderates*. New York: Oxford University Press.

Lotz, Anne Graham. 2000. *Just Give Me Jesus*. Nashville: Word Publishing.

Lucado, Max. 2009. *Fearless: Imagine Your Life Without Fear*. Nashville: Thomas Nelson.

MacNutt, Francis. 2009. *Healing (Orig Pub 1974)*. Notre Dame: Ave Maria Press.

Marshall, Alfred. 1956. *Principles of Economics: An Introductory Volume*. London: MacMillan.

Marx, Karl. 1843. *Critique of Hegel's Philosophy of Right (Zur Kritik der Hegelschen Rechtsphilosophie)*. Deutsch–Französische Jahrbücher. (Online: https://en.wikipedia.org/wiki/Opium_of_the_people)

Maslow, Abraham H. (1943). "*A Theory of Human Motivation*." Psychological Review. 50 (4): 370–96.

May, Gerald G. 1988. *Addiction & Grace: Love and Spirituality in the Healing of Addictions*. New York: HarperOne.

Mason, Karen. 2014. *Preventing Suicide: A Handbook for Pastors, Chaplains, and Pastoral Counselors*. Downers Grove: IVP Books.

McGrath, Alister. 2004. *The Twilight of Atheism: The Rise and Fall of Disbelief in the Modern World*. New York: DoubleDay.

Meinecke, Friedrich. 1969. *The German Catastrophe: The Social and Historical Influences Which Led to the Rise and Ruin of Hitler and Germany (Orig pub 1950)*. Translated by Sidney B. Fay. Boston: Beacon Press.

Metaxas, Eric. 2010. *Bonhoeffer: Pastor, Martyr, Prophet, Spy*. Nashville: Thomas Nelson.

Metzger, Bruce M. and Bart D. Ehrman. 2005. *The Text of the New Testament: Its Transmission, Corruption, and Restoration*. New York: Oxford University Press.

Miller, William R. and Stephen Rollnick. 2002. *Motivational Interviews: Preparing People for Change*. New York: Guilford Press.

Mishel, Lawrence. 2013. *Vast majority of wage earners are working harder, and for not much more: Trends in U.S.* work hours and wages over 1979–2007. Economic Policy Institute. January 30. Online: https://www.epi.org/publication/ib348-trends-us-work-hours-wages-1979-2007. Accessed: 26 November 2018.

Mischel, Walter. 2014. *The Marshmallow Test: Mastering Self-Control.* New York: Little, Brown and Company.

Montenegro, Marcia. 2006. *Spellbound: The Paranormal Seduction of Today's Kids.* Colorado Springs: Life Journey.

Moore, Russell. 2015. *Onward: Engaging the Culture without Losing the Gospel.* Nashville: B & H Publishing Group.

Myers, Isabel Briggs and Peter B. Myers. 1995. *Gifts Differing: Understanding Personality Type* (Orig Pub 1980). Mountain View: Davies-Black Publishing.

Nagel, Thomas. 2012. *What is It Like to Be a Bat? Mortal Questions, Canto Classics.* Cambridge: Cambridge University Press.

National Institute of Mental Health (NIH). 2018. *Any Anxiety Disorder.* Online: https://www.nimh.nih.gov/health/statistics/any-anxiety-disorder.shtml. Accessed: 26 November 2018.

Niebuhr, H. Richard. 1937. *The Kingdom of God in America*. New York: Harper Torchbooks.

Noll, Mark A. 2002. *The Work We Have to Do: A History of Protestants in America*. New York: Oxford University Press.

Nouwen, Henri J. M. 1975. *Reaching Out: The Three Movements of the Spiritual Life*. New York: DoubleDay.

Nouwen, Henri J. M. 2002. *In the Name of Jesus: Reflections on Christian Leadership*. New York: Crossroad Publishing Company.

Nouwen, Henri J.M. 2010. *Wounded Healer: Ministry in Contemporary Society* (Orig Pub 1972). New York: Image Doubleday.

NOVA. 2017. "*The Day the Dinosaurs Died.*" 27 December. Online: https://www.pbs.org/wgbh/nova/video/day-the-dinosaurs-died. Accessed: 18 January 2019.

Oden, Thomas C. 1992. *Two Worlds: Notes on the Death of Modernity in America and Russia*. Downers Grove: InterVarsity Press.

Ortberg, John. 2015. *All the Places to Go—How Will You Know? God has Placed Before You an Open Door: What Will You Do? Carol Stream: Tyndale House Publishers, Inc.*

Packer, J.I. 1993. *Knowing God*. Downers Grove: InterVarsity Press.

Payne, B. Keith. 2006. *"Weapon Bias: Split-Second Decisions and Unintended Stereotyping."* Sage Journals. December 1. Online: https://journals.sagepub.com/doi/10.1111/j.1467-8721.2006.00454.x. Accessed: 27 November 2018.

Patterson, Kerry Joseph Grenny, Ron McMillan, and Al Switzler. 2012. *Crucial Conversations: Tools for Talking When Stakes Are High*. New York: McGraw-Hill.

Pew Research Center. 2015. *The American Family Today*. December 17. Online: http://www.pewsocialtrends. org/2015/12/17/1-the-american-family-today. Accessed: 10 December 2018.

Phillips, John Bertram. 1997. *Your God is Too Small (Orig Pub 1953)*. New York: Simon & Schuster; A Touchstone Book.

Philips, Kevin. 2002. *Wealth and Democracy: A Political History of the American Rich*. New York: Broadway Books.

Placher, William C. 1989. *Unapologetic Theology: A Christian Voice in a Pluralistic Conversation*. Louisville: Westminster John Knox Press.

Plantinga, Alvin. 2000. *Warranted Christian Belief*. New York: Oxford University Press.

Polanyi, Michael. 1962. *Personal Knowledge: Towards a Post-Critical Philosophy*. Chicago: University of Chicago Press.

Porter, Michael E. 1980. *Competitive Strategy: Techniques for Analyzing Industries and Competitors*. New York: Free Press.

Presbyterian Church in the United States of America (PC USA). 1999. *The Constitution of the Presbyterian Church (U.S.A.)*—Part I: Book of Confession. Louisville, KY: Office of the General Assembly.

Ratzinger, Cardinal Joseph. 1994. *Catechism of the Catholic Church*. Preface by Pope John Paul II. Liguori: Liguori Publications.

Robinson, Haddon W. 2001. *Biblical Preaching: The Development and Delivery of Expository Messages*. Grand Rapids: Baker Academic.

Robson, David. 2013. *"There really are 50 Eskimo words for 'snow."* abstracted from New Scientist by the Washington Post. January 14. Online: https://www.washingtonpost.com/national/health-science/there-really-are-50-eskimo-words-for-snow/2013/01/14/e0e3f4e0-59a0-11e2-beee-6e38f5215402_story.html?utm_term=.f6d48a24e3f7. Accessed: 27 November 2018.

Rogers, Jack. 2009. *Jesus, The Bible, and Homosexuality: Explode the Myths, Heal the Church*. Louisville: Westminster John Knox Press.

Rosen, Sidney. 1982. *My Voice Will Go with You: The Teaching Tales of Milton H*. Erickson. New York: W.W. Norton.

Rosenthal, Alan. 2011. "Eichmann Revisited." The Jerusalem Post. April 20. Online: https://www.jpost.com/Jerusalem-Report/Jewish-World/Eichmann-Revisited. Accessed: December 3, 2018.

Sacks, Jonah. 2012. *Winning the Story Wars: Why Those Who Tell—and Live—the Best Stories Will Rule the Future*. Boston: Harvard Business School Press.

Sanders, E.P. 1993. *The Historical Figure of Jesus*. New York: Penguin Books.

Savage, John. 1996. *Listening & Caring Skills: A Guide for Groups and Leaders*. Nashville: Abingdon Press.

Schaeffer, Francis A. 2005. *How Should We Then Live: The Rise and Decline of Western Thought and Culture (Orig Pub 1976)*. Wheaton: Crossway Books.

Schmemann, Alexander. 1973. *For the Life of the World: Sacraments and Orthodoxy*. Crestwood: St. Vladimir's Seminary Press.

Schultz, Richard L. 2012. *Out of Context: How to Avoid Misinterpreting the Bible*. Grand Rapids: Baker Books.

Scientific American. 2018. *"Life Expectancy."* Online: https://www.scientificamerican.com/article/life-expectancy. Accessed: 24 November.

Sedniew, Andreii. 2013. *Magic of Impromptu Speaking: Create a Speech that Will Be Remembered for Years in Under 30 Seconds*. Santa Clara: Andreii Sedniev.

Shafer-Landau, Russ. 2018. *The Fundamentals of Ethics*. New York: Oxford University Press.

Bainton, Roland H. 1995. *Here I Stand: A Life of Martin Luther*. New York: Penguin.

Simon, Herbert A. 1997. *Administrative Behavior: A Study of Decision-Making Processes in Administrative Organizations (Orig Pub 1945)*. New York: Free Press.

Skinner, B.F. *1972*. Beyond Freedom and Dignity. New York: Bantam Books.

Smith, Houston. 2001. *Why Religion Matters: The Fate of the Human Spirit in an Age of Disbelief*. San Francisco: Harper.

Smith, James K.A. 2006. *Who's Afraid of Postmodernism: Taking Derrida, Lyotard, and Foucault to Church*. Grand Rapids: Baker Academic.

Smith, James K. A. 2016. *You Are What You Love: The Spiritual Power of Habit*. Grand Rapids: Brazos Press.

Sproul, R.C. 1977. *Knowing Scripture*. Downers Grove: InterVarsity Press.

Sproul, R.C. 1997. *What is Reformed Theology? Understanding the Basics*. Grand Rapids: BakerBooks.

Stanford, Matthew S. 2008. *Grace for the Afflicted: Viewing Mental Illness Through the Eyes of Faith*. Colorado Springs: Paternoster.

Stanton, Thomas H. 2012. *Why Some Firms Thrive While Others Fail: Governance and Management Lessons from the Crisis*. New York: Oxford University Press.

Stinnett, Nick and Nancy Stinnett, Joe Beam, and Alice Beam (Stinnett and Beam). 1999. *Fantastic Families: 6 Proven Steps to Building a Strong Family*. New York: Howard Books.

Stone, Larry. 2010. *The Story of the Bible: The Fascinating History of Its Writing, Translation, and Effect on Civilization*. Nashville: Thomas Nelson.

Strobel, Lee. 2016. *The Case for Christ: A Journalist's Personal Investigation of the Evidence for Jesus (Orig Pub 1998)*. Grand Rapids: Zondervan.

Swinburne, Richard. 1979. *The Existence of God*. Oxford: Clarendon Press.

Tavernise, Sabrina. 2016. "U.S. Suicide Rate Surges to a 30-Year High." New York Times. April 22. Online: https://nyti.ms/2k9vzFZ, Accessed: 13 March 2017.

Thompson, James W. 2011. *Moral Formation According to Paul*. Grand Rapids: Baker Academic.

Thurman, Howard. 1996. *Jesus and the Disinherited (Orig Pub 1949)*. Boston: Beacon Press.

Thurow, Lester C. 1975. *Generating Inequality*. New York: Basic Books.

Tozer, A. W. *2014*. Knowledge of the Holy: The Attributes of God. North Fort Myers: Faithful Life Publishers.

Turkle, Sherry. 2011. *Alone Together: Why we Expect More from Technology and Less from Each Other*. New York: Basic Books.

Van Broekhoven, Rollin A. 2017. "Morality And Law In A Global Society: A Place For Natural Law Theory?" Frontiers of Law in China. Vol 12:4. December.

Vanhoozer, Kevin J. 1998. Is There a Meaning in This Text: The Bible, The Reader, and the Morality of Literary Knowledge. Grand Rapids: Zondervan.

Vanhoozer, Kevin J. 2014. *Faith Speaking Understanding: Performing the Drama of Doctrine*. Louisville: Westminster John Knox Press.

Veith, Gene Edward, Jr. 1994. *Postmodern Times: A Christian Guide to Contemporary Thought and Culture*. Wheaton: Crossway Books.

Wallace, Gregory. 2015. "*Brands that Love LGBT the Most*." CNN Business. 12 January. Online: https://money.cnn.com/2015/01/12/news/companies/lgbt-brands/index.html. Accessed: 8 January 2019.

Webb, William J. 2001. *Slaves, Women, and Homosexuals: Exploring the Hermeneutics of Cultural Analysis*. Downers Grove: IVP Press.

Wemm, Stephanie E. and Edelgard Wulfert. *2017*. "Effects of Acute Stress on Decision Making." Pp 1-12 in Applied Psychophysiology and Biofeedback. 42:1. March. Online: https://www.ncbi.nlm.nih.gov/pmc/articles/PMC5346059. Accessed 27 November 2018.

Whelchel, Hugh. 2012. *How Then Should We Work? Rediscovering the Biblical Doctrine of Work*. Bloomington: WestBow Press.

Whitaker, Bill. 2017. *"Ex-DEA agent: Opioid crisis fueled by drug industry and Congress."* 17 October. Online: https://www.cbsnews.com/news/ex-dea-agent-opioid-crisis-fueled-by-drug-industry-and-congress. Accessed: 15 January 2019.

White, James Emery. 2004. *Serious Times: Making Your Life Matter in an Urgent Day*. Downers Grove: InterVarsity Press.

Wilberforce, William. 2006. *A Practical View of Christianity (Orig Pub 1797)*. Ed. Kevin Charles Belmonte. Peabody, MA: Hendrickson Christian Classics; Hendrickson Publishers.

Williamson, Oliver. 1981. *"The Modern Corporation: Origin, Evolution, Attributes."* pp. 1537-1568 in Journal of Economic Literature. December.

Wilson, James Q. and George L. Kelling. 1982. *"Broken Windows: The Police and Neighborhood Safety."* Atlantic Monthly. March.

Wolters, Albert M. 2005. *Creation Regained: Biblical Basics for a Reformation Worldview*. Grand Rapids: Eerdmans.

Yancey, Philip. 2002. *Where is God When It Hurts? Grand Rapids: Zondervan.*

Zezima, Katie and Seung Min Kim. 2018 *"Trump signs sweeping opioid bill. Expect to hear about it on the campaign trail."* Washington Post. October 24, Online: https://www.washingtonpost.com/politics/trump-signs-sweeping-opioid-bill-expect-to-hear-about-it-on-the-campaign-trail/2018/10/24/1328598c-d7a9-11e8-aeb7-ddcad4a0a54e_story.html?utm_term=.5b81f5c6b2e4. Accessed: 15 January 2019.

SCRIPTURAL INDEX

Revelation

ABOUT

*A*uthor Stephen W. Hiemstra lives in Centreville, VA with Maryam, his wife of more than thirty years. Together, they have three grown children.

Stephen worked as an economist for twenty-seven years in more than five federal agencies, where he published numerous government studies, magazine articles, and book reviews. He wrote his first book, *A Christian Guide to Spirituality* in 2014. In 2015, he translated and published a Spanish edition, *Una Guía Cristiana a la Espiritualidad*. In 2016, he wrote a second book, *Life in Tension*, which also focuses on Christian spirituality. In 2017, he published a memoir, *Called Along the Way*. In 2018, he published a *Spiritual Trilogy* (an eBook compilation) and his first hardcover book, *Everyday Prayers for Everyday People*.

Stephen has a Masters of Divinity (MDiv, 2013) from Gordon-Conwell Theological Seminary in Charlotte, NC. His doctorate (PhD, 1985) is in agricultural economics from Michigan State. He studied in Puerto Rico and Germany, and speaks Spanish and German.

Correspond with Stephen at T2Pneuma@gmail.com or follow his blog at http://www.T2Pneuma.net.

Made in the USA
Middletown, DE
01 May 2019